Prague

Berlitz Publishing Company, Inc.
Princeton   Mexico City   London   Eschborn   Singapore

Copyright © 2001 Berlitz Publishing Company, Inc.
400 Alexander Park, Princeton, NJ, 08540 USA
9-13 Grosvenor St., London, W1K 4QA UK

Berlitz Trademark Reg. U.S. Patent Office and other countries
Marca Registrada

Text:	Lindsay Bennett
Editor:	Media Content Marketing, Inc.
Photography:	Pete Bennett
Cover Photo:	Pete Bennett
Photo Editor:	Naomi Zinn
Layout:	Media Content Marketing, Inc.
Cartography:	Ortelius Design

Although the publisher tries to insure the accuracy of all the information in this book, changes are inevitable and errors may result. The publisher cannot be responsible for any resulting loss, inconvenience, or injury. If you find an error in this guide, please let the editors know by writing to Berlitz Publishing Company, 400 Alexander Park, Princeton, NJ 08540-6306.

ISBN 2-8315-7704-7

Printed in Italy
010/103 REV

CONTENTS

● A (☞ in the text denotes a highly recommended sight

Prague

THE CITY
AND ITS PEOPLE

In the 21st century, the itinerary is king. We plan every detail of our busy lives to fit in as much as we can. This is certainly true when we take a vacation. World travel has become easy and inexpensive, and there's a temptation to make a whistle-stop tour simply to tick off as many destinations as possible: a sort of "been there, done that" attitude. However, even in our world of "virtual reality," some destinations still have a capacity to give even the most cynical tourist pause for thought. They refuse to be reduced to a mere list of museums or galleries. Prague is one of these destinations. Its beauty is truly breathtaking and its unique character has been developed over many centuries as an important and influential capital city.

Set on the banks of the Vltava River (a tributary of the Elbe), the site was chosen both for its strategic setting and its beauty. The heart of the old city nestles in a bowl surrounded by rolling hills. Czech folklore tells of a Princess Libuše who had a premonition about a shining city and the exact spot where it should be founded. She married a common plough-man or *přemysl* to beget the first ruling dynasty, and her descendents were credited with being true and just.

Sitting in the heart of Europe — perhaps a little further north and west than most people think — Prague (Praha in Czech) has been the capital of the ancient realm of Bohemia for centuries. During the Middle Ages it rose to prominence as the capital of Charles IV's vast empire. As Holy Roman Emperor and ruler of much of Western Europe, he was probably the most powerful man in the world at the time (1316–1378). In the 16th century the city was a leading center in the Hapsburg court and it became capital of the newly independent country of Czechoslovakia in 1918. During the late 20th century the Czech Republic chafed under the yoke of Communist rule, but when the Iron Curtain fell in 1989, Prague unveiled its hidden wealth of Bohemian treasures and sent out an invitation to the rest of the world.

The city presents a unique architectural tapestry with a rich pattern created through the legacies of generations. Intricately detailed and created with exquisite workmanship, it is decorated with Gothic, Renaissance, Baroque, and Art Nouveau gems. The fabric has been interwoven with political and religious intrigue, and stitched together by the rich seam of work by master architects, painters, sculptors, and musicians.

Pride of place must go to Prague Castle, the seat of royal power through the Middle Ages, which sits majestically atop a low ridge and casts a watchful eye over the happenings of the city. Royal patronage spawned a court, which in turn attracted the rich and powerful like a magnet. These families spent fortunes building fine mansions and summer palaces, decorating them with creations by the finest artisans of their time. The church also played its part, but in Bohemia this was complicated because it was a major battleground between adherents of Catholicism and church reformers. The many impressive cathedrals, churches, chapels, convents, and monasteries erected here attest to the vehemence of the struggle — and the eventual triumph of the Catholic Church — giving Prague the epithet "city of one hundred spires."

The dramatic urban landscape changes with every passing hour, subject to the constantly changing clouds and the movement of the sun across the sky. In the mornings, gentle fresh light washes over statuary and domes, and towards sunset heavy, syrupy rays ripen the pastel stucco and gilded shopping opportunities. It is also one of the architectural highlights of the city. A large, somewhat irregular shape, which has changed over the centuries, it is dominated in modern times by a powerful **monument to Jan Hus** (Pomník Jana Husa) unveiled in 1915 on the 500th anniversary of the martyr's death.

The **Old Town Hall** (Staroměstská radnice) sits on the southwestern corner of the square. A curious amalgamation of several buildings in different architectural styles — its earliest elements are 14th century — it expanded as Prague developed in importance. Badly damaged in WWII, the east wing has only recently been restored.

The astronomical clock on the Old Town Hall provides an unusual show each hour.

Although there are many interesting features on the exterior of the building, most visitors crowd to see the **astronomical clock**, which was added in 1490. It was so highly prized at the time by the city fathers that they had the clockmaker who made it stricken blind so that he could not recreate his masterpiece. At the top of every hour the figures on the clock perform their ritual. Death consults his watch and pulls a cord that rings a bell; Christ and the apostles appear above, and the crow of a cock signals the end of the proceedings. The clock marks time from the passing seconds to the cycles of the sun and moon. Don't forget that according to this model, the earth is the center of the universe.

You can tour the interior of the Old Town Hall to see the council chambers with their superb tapestries, the newly renovated Oriel Chapel, and climb the **Old Town Hall Tower** erected in 1364, from where you can get an excellent view of the surrounding streets and rooftops. Abutting the Old Town Hall is **Dům U Minuty**. With its distinctive *sgraffito* decoration it is one of the most memorable Renaissance buildings in Prague.

The western flank of the square has altered dramatically in the late 20th century. A large open area behind the Old Town Hall was created following the destruction meted out during the German occupation. It now has numerous craft stalls, and benches where weary tourists can take a rest. The ornate façade of the **Church of St. Nicholas** (Kostel svatého Mikuláše) was once hidden down a narrow side street but today it forms part of the northern flank. Though there has been a church on this site since the 12th century, this present building dates from 1735. During World War I it was taken over by troops of the Prussian army as a barracks and at the end of the conflict was handed over to the Hussite Church. It now acts as a concert venue in the summer season.

The eastern flank is dominated by two buildings. The splendid rococo façade belongs to **Golz-Kinský Palace** (Palác Golz-Kinských) designed by Kilian Deintzenhofer and built by Anselmo Lurago for the Golz family in 1768. In 1948 Klement Gottwald made a speech from the balcony of the palace, which was instrumental in the Communist takeover of the government. The neighboring building could not be more of a contrast to the ornate rococo features of Golz-Kinský. The arcaded entrance portal to the **Church of Our Lady before Týn** (Kostel Panny Marie před Týnem)

Beyond the river Vltava and into the heart of Prague, there is a sprawling, beautiful city to explore.

spires to give a radiant golden hue. Passing seasons also introduce a different atmosphere. Though there is no doubt that Prague looks beautiful on a bright summer day, it is equally enchanting surrounded by the copper tints of fall, or blanketed by a veneer of crisp winter snow.

The nightscape is no less disappointing, with artificial light bathing a myriad of buildings. The shimmering reflections on the Vltava River, and the waxy glow of thousands of streetlights are two reasons why Prague is considered to be one of the world's most romantic cities. It was this air of romance that inspired Mozart, Beethoven, and leading Czech composers Dvořák and Smetena, along with numerous visual artists. Today it still inspires professional painters and photographers as well as thousands of amateur enthusiasts.

Centuries of the best in music, theater and art encouraged a cultured and urbane society; the people of Prague appreciate their theaters and galleries as much as visitors do, revelling in the artistic legacy of the Hapsburg years and the flourish of artistic endeavors that accompanied their growing nationalism in the 19th century. Tickets for concerts and other performances in the city are deliberately kept low to allow local people, whatever their walk of life, to avail themselves of the unrivalled concert season. However, they don't spend all of their time in highbrow pursuits. Don't forget that the Czech Republic is one of the world's leading beer producers, and local folks are equally at home having a few drinks in the beer halls around the city, or spending the late night hours in a smoky jazz club or rock bar. The angst-ridden café society which gave rise to the writings of Franz

The streets of Prague come alive throughout the year with music and celebrations of the traditional culture.

Kafka, or the cubist art of the Group of Visual Artists in the early 20th century can still be found, though you are much more likely to find people enjoying ice cream than discussing philosophy, perhaps taking the air in one of many areas of parkland, or driving around town in the all-pervading Czech-produced Skoda car.

Of course there have been many changes since 1989 for both the city and its people. The younger generation has grown up with the kinds of freedom taken for granted by teenagers in the west. They throng to the western boutiques to buy the latest fashions or pop CDs, and carry the ubiquitous mobile phone everywhere. However, at a time when one can set almost any ringer tone to personalize a phone, the fact that so many in Prague select the haunting lilts of traditional Slavic melodies is one indication that they have not left their roots behind.

The Czech economy has been buoyed greatly by the increase in visitor numbers during the 1990s, and it has allowed many historic buildings to benefit from a massive renovation program that fills the streets of certain parts of the city with a smell of paint and damp stucco. You will certainly find it difficult to avoid your fellow travelers, be they honeymooning couples strolling hand in hand along the narrow lanes, students on a budget European "culture-fest," or large tour groups tramping en masse across the city squares. That Prague manages to satisfy the disparate demands of all these people attests to its diversity. There are very few places where you can view a saint's tomb, ponder over the work of several European masters, climb a 14th-century tower, take a carriage ride or a river cruise, bargain over the price of exquisite crystal, take a romantic evening stroll, and enjoy a classical concerto, all within the space of a few hours. Prague allows you to do this — and a little more.

A BRIEF HISTORY

Prague has had an illustrious history throughout the Christian era. It has been at the heart of power within one of the major European dynasties — the Austro-Hungarian. Figures as distinguished as Good King Wenceslas, Holy Roman Emperor Charles IV, Jan Hus, and the Hapsburg family feature prominently in its story. However the city has also seen political and religious oppression, intrigue, and murder as the machinations of the power brokers were played out, resulting in as many sad as happy times.

Located at a natural fording place on the Vltava River, which is linked with the River Elbe, Prague was settled as early as the Stone Age. Remains, including tools and jewels, have been found in the area. Celtic tribesmen settled here well over two thousand years ago, followed by a Germanic people. However, of more lasting significance, the first Slavs — ancestors of the Czechs — arrived in the fifth or sixth century A.D., choosing to settle on the hilltops for safety.

The second half of the ninth century saw the construction of the original fortifications of the castle. It was from here that the Czechs were ruled by the members of the Přemyslid family, a dynasty going back to mythical roots and forward well into the Middle Ages.

A Saintly Pioneer

Methodius, a Greek preacher, has been credited for bringing Christianity to the Slavs during the late ninth century. He baptized Prince Borivoj and his wife Ludmilla circa 873. Methodius went on to be declared a true saint, as did Ludmilla. Following her assassination she was proclaimed patron saint of Bohemia. The grandson of Ludmilla, the first of the rulers named Wenceslas (*Václav* in Czech), held the crown in the tenth century. During his reign a church dedicated to St. Vitus was built at Prague Castle. Wenceslas, who was a fervent believer, became the first of the Czech princes to be murdered on the job — he was ambushed on his way to mass. It was a family affair in the classic mold; the killer was his younger brother, Boleslav.

Far from being condemned for eliminating the now sainted Wenceslas, Boleslav assumed power and held it for nearly half a century. During his long reign a well-traveled Jewish merchant, Ibrahim ibn Jacob, wrote admiringly of Prague

Good King Wenceslas, now sainted, sits high above the square that bears his name.

as a great and busy trading center with solid buildings of stone. The town became a bishopric in 973, at about the time that the monastery of St. George was established on Castle Hill.

Early on in the 11th century Přemyslid rule was extended to neighboring Moravia by Břetislav I, the great-grandson of Boleslav. He went on to become a vassal of the German emperor, opening the door to centuries of German influence. Břetislav's son, Vratislav II, was the first monarch to bear the title of King of Bohemia.

More Wenceslases

Prince Wenceslas I, the saint, was not the only Wenceslas I. The second Wenceslas I became King of Bohemia in 1230, and ruled long and well. Encouraging the arts, he presided over a growing prosperity — and population. Since the early 13th century, immigrants from Germany had been moving into Bohemia and some settled in Prague. In 1257, King Otakar II founded the Lesser Quarter as a German enclave, protected by German law. Under Wenceslas II, Otakar's son, the economy boomed thanks to large finds of silver, and the Prague *groschen* became a stable international currency.

The dynasty's luck eventually ran out with the son of Wenceslas II. In the summer of 1306, early in his reign, the teenage king Wenceslas III went down in history as the last of the Přemyslid kings when he was assassinated in Moravia.

The Great Charles

Another Wenceslas grew up to be the king who transformed Prague from a provincial town into an important world capital. He was the son of John (Jan) of Luxembourg, who ruled Bohemia for 36 years, and after gaining a good education in Paris, this prince chose to change his name to Charles.

Even before his coronation, the future King, Charles IV, was deeply involved in running Prague and Bohemia. His relations with the church were always warm, and in 1344 he convinced the pope to promote Prague to an archbishopric. Under his direction, centuries of work began on the present St. Vitus Cathedral, the resplendent Gothic centerpiece of Hradčany Castle. Early in his reign Charles acted to put Prague firmly on the intellectual map of the world by founding Central Europe's first university in 1348. He expanded the city to the New Town, thus providing room for useful immigrants from all over Europe — artists, craftsmen, and merchants. Finally, he gave Prague its Gothic bridge, the Charles Bridge, which is still a useful and beautiful link between the Old Town and Lesser Quarter after more than 600 years.

In 1355 Charles added yet another historic title to his regalia when he was crowned Holy Roman Emperor. Back in Prague he ruled nobly over the empire, as well as Bohemia, until his death in 1378.

Religious Strife

The city of Prague should have thrived as the administrative headquarters of the empire that Charles had consolidated, but people and events conspired against it. Charles IV's son and successor, Wenceslas IV, turned out to be a most irresolute leader. He turned his back on feuds, revolts, and wars and was eventually deposed.

In the most momentous crisis that Wenceslas failed to address, Prague lived through the first skirmishes of a prelude

---

Architecture in a nutshell

The constant reference to architectural periods can be confusing, especially in a destination as rich in historic buildings as Prague. For those who are unsure of which periods relate to which dates, here is a list of the major phases (though dates are general, as eras do overlap or have transitional phases).

Romanesque	c1000–1140
Gothic	c1140 to the mid-16th century. One of the last European Gothic structures dates from the1530s.
Renaissance	c1400s to the 1600s
Baroque	c1600s to the 1750s
Rococo	1715 to 1774 and linked to the era of Louis XIV in France
Art Nouveau	c1880s to the first decade of the 20th century
Modernist	from the turn of the 20th century

---

to the Reformation. At Bethlehem Chapel in the old Town, a priest, theologian, and professor named Jan Hus challenged the excesses of the Catholic Church of the day and demanded it change its ways. Hus's demands for reform became so vigorous that he was excommunicated, then arrested for heresy, and finally burned at the stake in 1415, but not before he had built up a large and loyal following. In the aftermath of his martyrdom, the Hussite movement (as it became known), went marching on with ever wider popular support, much to the dismay of the Papacy. In 1419 a reformist mob invaded Prague's New Town Hall, liberated imprisoned Hussites, and threw several Catholic city councilors from the windows. History calls this event the First Defenestration of Prague. It was to be the start of a long tradition.

The harried brother of the unfortunate Wenceslas, King Sigismund, marshaled Czech Catholic forces and foreign allies in a crusade against the Hussites. The rebels, however, fought back. Their under-equipped but highly motivated peasant army won some noteworthy victories, defeating Sigismund at the Battle of Vítkov Hill. The rebels were commanded by a brilliant one-eyed soldier, Jan Žižka, but following his death the leadership foundered and eventually the rebels were defeated. Their saga is still richly remembered today in the Czech Republic.

Sigismund died without leaving a successor. He was followed by his son-in-law Albrecht of Austria, and then Albrecht's son, Ladislas; both of whom had short reigns. A dynamic politician by the name of George of Poděbrady, who was implicated in the death of Ladislav, was elected to succeed him. George aligned himself with the Hussites, to the great displeasure of the neighboring Catholic kings and the papacy. He was eventually excommunicated and boycotted, as was Prague by the international diplomatic and business community.

Four Hapsburg Centuries

Absentee kings ruled Bohemia from George's death until 1526, when the Hapsburgs claimed the throne. This dynasty held sway over what remained of the Holy Roman Empire and their attention was taken with protecting their European borders against the very real Moslem threat. Bohemia's grave religious divisions were simply another thorn in their side. By now the Protestant faith had become a powerful influence and the Hapsburgs remained zealous Catholics.

Knights of the Cross Square holds a statue of the Holy Roman Emperor, Charles IV.

In 1576 Emperor Rudolph II came to the throne and made the remarkable decision to move his capital from Vienna to Prague. Under this imperial impulse the arts and sciences reached new heights, and splendid Renaissance buildings further beautified the city. The principal accomplishment of his reign was a decree that granted freedom of religion to all Catholics and Protestants alike. However, the Catholic king, Ferdinand II, who came to the throne in 1611, did not honor it. This served to exacerbate the inherent religious conflict, which soon escalated into the suffering of the pan-European Thirty Years' War.

The people of Prague witnessed numerous defenestrations — bodies flung from a window in the Bohemian Chancellery

During the 18th century, Prague was graced by many elaborate homes, such as the stately Troja Palace.

of Prague Castle. In the rebellion that ensued, Ferdinand was deposed, but his supporters rallied and, triumphed in the Battle of the White Mountain, fought on Prague's doorstep in 1620. Restored to power, Ferdinand sent persuasive messages about loyalty to the populace: he had a couple of dozen rebel leaders executed in the Old Town Square and proclaimed Roman Catholicism the only legal religion.

Ferdinand's decisive victory radically changed the face of Prague, haggard as it was after the fighting. A large majority of Protestant landowners emigrated, and their property went to Ferdinand's Catholic supporters. Baroque architecture, typical of the sort favored in Catholic Italy, became the fashion, and the medieval atmosphere of Prague gave way to grand, extravagant 17th-century palaces. Numerous new churches signaled the great triumph of the Counter-Reformation. Henceforward,

German, not Czech, was spoken in the palace and courthouse. The tensions that grew up between Prague's German and Czech-speaking citizens would persist well into the 20th century.

Maria Theresa, the daughter, wife, and mother of Holy Roman emperors, was the only queen to have reigned over Prague. In between diplomatic engagements she produced 16 children, including Marie Antoinette, the future Queen of France. Under her son and heir, Joseph II, religious toleration was restored. Joseph also abolished serfdom and relaxed censorship. On the municipal level, he consolidated the city of Prague from its previous four components — Hradčany, Lesser Quarter, Old Town, and New Town. Music provides a gauge of the cultural development of Joseph's Prague: in 1787 Mozart was invited to conduct the world premiere of *Don Giovanni* in the Estates Theater, where it was a huge success.

Industrial Prague

By the middle of the 19th century, Prague's population exceeded 100,000. Factories were built and a railway line to Vienna was opened, signaling the start of the Industrial Revolution. Bohemia went on to become the most advanced manufacturing center of the Austrian Empire.

Another kind of revolution started in 1848, uniting Czech nationalists and the new working class of Prague against the overlords in Vienna. The remote, rigid Austrian authorities soon extinguished the uprising, but not the smoldering nationalist feelings of the Czechs. When Prague's monumental National Theater opened in 1881, the first work ever performed was a new opera by Smetana, a proud and patriotic saga called *Libuše*. Dvořák, too, took his inspiration from Czech folk songs. Nationalist Prague was conspicuously out-of-step with the rhythm of the Hapsburg capital, Vienna, the home of the waltz.

The 20th Century

When the heir to the Hapsburg throne, Archduke Franz Ferdinand, was assassinated in June 1914, the Austro-Hungarian Empire was plunged into the tragic carnage of World War I. From the dusty ashes of the defeated Austria-Hungary, an independent Czechoslovakian republic was proclaimed in October 1918. Prague was the capital of the First Republic, comprising Bohemia, Moravia, and Slovakia. The first president was Tomáš G. Masaryk, a widely traveled and admired philosophy professor, who was re-elected three times. He died in 1937, before the agony of yet another European war.

Czechoslovakia was at the center of the storm that blew up into World War II. In September 1938, Hitler demanded self-determination for Czechoslovakia's German-speaking citizens. To try to appease him, Britain and France handed over the country's western provinces. Then Hitler threatened to rain bombs on Prague unless the remains of the country were made a German protectorate. The government of what remained of Czechoslovakia's Second Republic capitulated. Six long years of occupation were to follow before Soviet troops liberated the city in May 1945.

When parliamentary elections were held a year later, the communists won nearly 40 percent of the votes. The non-communist pre-war president Edvard Beneš, elected again, invited the veteran communist leader Klement Gottwald to form a coalition cabinet.

Gottwald, who had spent the war years in the Soviet Union, seized his big chance in 1948. When several non-communist ministers resigned in protest against his one-sided policies, Gottwald packed the government with supporters. Non-communist foreign minister Jan Masaryk, son of Tomáš, was found dead below his office window at the foreign ministry. Speculation was rife that this was another defenestration.

Gottwald, as the new president, framed a five-year economic plan, cracked down on the churches, and purged his opponents outside and inside the party. Scores of political figures were executed, and thousands arrested. The show trials went on under Antonín Novotný, while farmers were forced into collectives and the arts were smothered under harsh Socialist Realism.

A reform movement in the late 1960s culminated in the "Prague Spring" under Alexander Dubček, the head of the Slovak communist party. Unshackling the press and the arts, Dubček promised "socialism with a human face." But this was 20 years too early. On 21 August 1968, reform was crushed by the armed forces of the Soviet Union, ostensibly there by invitation, and with assistance from Poland, Bulgaria, East Germany, and Hungary. As the rest of the world watched massive Soviet tanks rumbling through Wenceslas Square, Prague wept. The new party chiefs returned to hard-line traditions even when the winds of change finally blew in from Moscow in the form of perestroika.

St. Nicholas Church is but one symbol of Prague's long religious history.

New Challenges

In 1989, Wenceslas Square was again the scene of repression: television showed the police clubbing peaceful students who demonstrated for an end to one-party rule. This time the long-suffering citizens had had enough and Prague's seemingly invincible communist regime simply folded before the people, and handed over its power. The playwright Václav Havel called it the "velvet revolution."

Dubček, rehabilitated, was elected chairman of a rejuvenated parliament. Meanwhile, Havel, freshly out of jail for dissident activities, was acclaimed the nation's president. In June 1992, parliamentary elections were won by the Civil Democratic Party and Václav Klaus became prime minister of the cabinet. In the meantime, Václav Havel renounced his position as federal president.

However in this first flush of freedom, old tensions between Czechs (including Moravians and Silesians) and Slovaks resurfaced, threatening a violent and damaging split within the country. Acutely aware of the social and political undercurrents, politicians dealt quickly with the problem by talking rather than fighting. On 1 January 1993, Czechoslovakia was peaceably divided into the Czech and Slovak Republics, and in February of that same year Václav Havel was returned to power as the President of the new Czech Republic with its capital in Prague.

Throughout the late 1990s, as the Czech Republic came to grips with democratic and capitalist reforms, Prague has seen an unprecedented influx of investment for renovation, and an exponential rise in visitor numbers. The major questions at the commencement of the new millennium is how the Czech people will manage their valuable and historic legacy in view of the city's popularity and the country's need to prosper in the free world.

WHERE TO GO

Prague is probably one of the most tourist-friendly cities in the world. Almost every corner reveals an architectural treasure dating from the 13th century to the present day, and numerous fine large mansions house impressive collections of art, folkloric artifacts, or musical masterpieces. The heart of the city can be walked across in one hour along a grid of traffic-free streets, yet there is an inexpensive and unobtrusive public transport system for those who would rather ride. Several tracts of land close to downtown are left green, where you can sit and enjoy the sunshine and birdsong.

This guide divides Prague into its traditional smaller settlements of Hradčany (the castle area), Lesser Quarter (Malá Strana), Old Town (Staré Město), and New Town (Nové Město). We'll point out the major historical and architectural highlights of each and also take time to enjoy the famed bridge that links the city across the Vltava River. We'll then move on to the surrounding suburbs of the city where there are attractions only a short metro or tram ride away. Finally, we'll travel outside the city to explore some of the day excursion destinations that can be reached from the city — either independently or with an organized tour.

HRADČANY (THE CASTLE DISTRICT)

The surprise of your first view of Prague Castle from across the Vltava River, is its vast size. Not for the Hapsburgs a simple stone stronghold: This citadel covers the area of a small town, and its numerous fine buildings make a real statement about royal power throughout the centuries. From its antecedents some 1,000 years ago, it developed to perform important ceremonial as well as protective functions. In the present day, part of the castle has been renovated to house the office of the President of the Czech Republic, continuing its leading role in diplomatic circles.

The castle was originally built here because sitting atop a ridge it had excellent views along the river valley and the town below. There are three entrances for today's visitors but we will enter from the ceremonial gate at the western side. This is the starting point of most guided tours and is the highest point of the castle complex. From here you will be walking downhill towards the eastern steps at the other side.

Before entering the castle take a look around **Hradčany Square** (Hradčanské náměstí), which forms an irregular open space outside the gates. Several important grand residences were built here in close proximity to the seat of power, and

The official palace guards stand at attention outside the gates of Prague Castle.

most of these have undergone a comprehensive restoration process during the 1990s. A small grassy area at the center of the square protects a plague column, erected by grateful survivors after an outbreak of the disease in the 18th century.

On the western side of the square is the **Tuscan Palace** (Toskánsky palác), a 17th-century Baroque residence, and its neighbor, the former **Martinic Palace** (Martinický palác), which is in earlier Renaissance style. It now hosts concerts in its main hall and inner courtyard, where renovations revealed *sgraffito* (patterns incised on a flat wall of plaster to create a 3D effect of shade and depth) depicting biblical scenes.

PRAGUE CASTLE (PRAŽSKÝ HRAD)

Across the park, **Schwarzenberg Palace** (Schwarzenberský palác) is perhaps the most distinctive building on the square. Each façade is covered with brick-like *sgraffito* and its effect is to link the disparate architectural styles of the palace into a coherent whole. The palace was built for the Lobkowicz family by Italian architect Agostini Galli in the mid 1500s, thus it has much more of a Florentine influence than other buildings of the time. Since 1945 the palace has housed the **Museum of Military History,** but has been undergoing extensive renovation.

The most ornate building on the square is the **Archbishop's Palace** (Arcibiskupský palác) sitting just beside the castle entrance. The house became the Archbishop's Palace following the Counter-Reformation in 1562 and its position was an indication of the power of the Catholic Church and its influence on the Hapsburg monarchy. The façade was redesigned in the 1760s in high-rococo style, its highlights brought out by a recent coat of paint. It is only open to the public on one day each year — Maundy Thursday (the Thursday before Easter).

Next door to this palace is one of the major art galleries of Prague, though a less auspicious entrance way is difficult to imagine. A narrow, cobbled alleyway leads to **Sternberg Palace** (Šternberský palác), home of Franz Sternberg who was a great patron of the arts during the late 18th century. The fine Baroque building now houses the Czech Republic's **National Gallery of European Art**, with a fine range of Old Masters dating from the 14th to the 18th century. Don't forget that the Hapsburgs and the Austro-Hungarian Empire that they ruled, of which Prague was a leading city, was the most powerful dynasty of its time. Their collection of art incorporates work by the finest artists of their respective eras. Flemish and Dutch art features particularly strongly with works by the Brueghel dynasty, along with Peter Paul Rubens, Rembrandt, and Frans Hals. Italian artists are represented with a wealth of 14th- and 15th-century decoration from churches in Tuscany. Later paintings feature the work of Tintoretto and El Greco. Perhaps the most noted painting in the collection is found in the Austrian and German section. Along with works by Hans Holbein and his son is *The Feast of the Rosary* by Albrecht Dürer, with two Hapsburg figures depicted on the canvas.

After visiting the gallery you may want to take a little break before exploring the castle proper. Just to the south of the castle gate there is a panoramic view over the city where you can

The Black Dog of Hradčany

According to legend, the ghost of a large black dog haunts the Hradčanské náměstí entrance to Prague Castle. It appears between 11pm and midnight, and far from being ferocious it accompanies strollers as far as the Loreto before disappearing into thin air.

catch your breath, and a few wonderful images with your camera. There's also a café where you can take refreshment.

The castle was begun in the 9th century and by the beginning of the 14th century housed the palace, churches, and a monastery. Refurbished during the reign of Charles IV, it was ravaged by fire in 1541 and most

> Take a pair of binoculars on your trip — you will see every detail of the amazing decoration.

of the buildings were reconstructed in the Renaissance style which was fashionable at the time. This created the unified appearance of many of the buildings within the castle walls. The castle eventually became a backwater as the Austro-Hungarian Empire chose to base itself permanently in Vienna, but it was thoroughly renovated in the early 1920s just after Czechoslovakia became independent. Surrounding the walls are many gardens offering a peaceful retreat from the sometimes crowded rooms and galleries within.

Enter the castle proper through ornate gates topped with heroic statues of fighting giants. Sombre uniformed guardsmen form silent sentinel as you pass through. This first courtyard — added in the 18th century — flanks **Matthias Gate** (Matyášova Brána), the entryway dating from 1614 that once formed a triumphal arch over moats (now filled in) leading to the second courtyard. Immediately ahead is the entrance to the **Holy Cross Chapel** (kaple svatého Kříže). Here you can find a fascinating collection of Holy relics and treasures accumulated by nearby St. Vitus Cathedral over the centuries.

On the northern flank of this courtyard the **Picture Gallery of Prague Castle** (Obrazárna Pražského Hradu) is housed in the former castle stables. The gallery displays artwork mainly collected by Rudolf II during his reign (1583–1612). He was passionate about art but much of his collection was taken to Vienna in the years after his reign or lost as booty to Swedish forces in 1648. Still the gallery boasts works by Tintoretto, Veronese, and Rubens. It is also possible for visitors to enter the north gardens through an archway here.

A narrow passage leads into the third courtyard of the castle and your view is immediately dominated by the immense and awe-inspiring façade of **St. Vitus Cathedral** (Katedrála svatého Víta) just a few steps away. The towers and spires dwarf the surrounding buildings and at first glance alter one's perception of scale. The cathedral acts as a reliquary for numerous national treasures and the bones of some of the Czech Republic's most famous and revered individuals. The first church on this hallowed ground was built in the 10th century by Prince Wenceslas, who was interred in the rotunda after his premature death. This present edifice was begun in 1344 when Prague was declared a bishopric. Charles IV decided that the new cathedral should be in the style of the great religious buildings of France and invited Matthias of Arras to design and build it. After Matthew's death, the work was continued by Peter Parler, a German architect, who in turn was followed by his two sons. Work was disrupted during the Hussite uprisings and was intermittent through the following centuries, in fact the whole building was not regarded as complete until 1929. The main entrance is now through the western doorway, but until the 19th century the southern door or Golden Portal was the entry way. The porch of this doorway is highly decorated and crowned with an ornate mosaic of the *Last Judgement*. To the left, a Gothic window is filled with delicate gold filigree work.

Once visitors enter the cathedral, the immense size is immediately apparent. There are over 18 separate chapels lining the walls. The 19th and 20th century element of the cathedral (near the main entrance) contains a chapel with stained glass by Alfons Mucha, greatly admired for his Art Nouveau artwork. However the eye automatically leads down the heart of the building to the magnificent chancel built by Parler in the 1370s. The towering vaults, decorated with delicate tracery, are a high point in Gothic architectural achievement. These are underpinned by ornate stained glass windows.

Several of the chapels in this area of the cathedral deserve further examination but none more so than that of **Wenceslas Chapel** (kaple svatého Václava), named for now Saint Wenceslas, or the

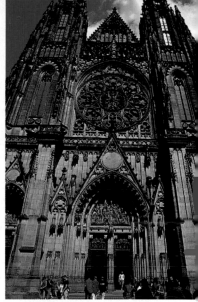

Behold the many treasures hidden behind the massive façade of St. Vitus Cathedral.

Good King Wenceslas of the Christmas carol. Parler created a wonderful Gothic room to house the tomb of the Prince, on the same spot as it had been in the previous Romanesque Rotunda. The walls are decorated with precious stones and gold leaf interspersed with several ornate frescoes illustrating scenes from the life of the saint. Behind the chapel is a small room containing the Coronation Jewels. Seven separate keys are needed to unlock the door to the chamber and the jewels remain out of view except for certain state occasions.

Next to the Wenceslas Chapel are stairs to the crypt where you can see the walls of earlier religious structures. This room holds the remains of Charles IV and members of his family, along with the tomb of Rudolph II. Above the crypt, in the main level of the cathedral, several other important rulers are interred. Ferdinand I lies in a large white marble tomb with his wife and son Maximilian. An ornate silver tomb holds the remains of Jan of Nepomuk, who was thrown from Charles Bridge in 1393 and made a saint in the early days of the Counter-Reformation.

To the north of the cathedral you will find **Powder Tower** (Mihulka), part of the 15th-century defensive walls but later used as a foundry and gunpowder workshop. Rumors

The 15th-century Powder Tower appears tiny with the great spires of St. Vitus Cathedral in the background.

abounded about experiments in alchemy taking place here, and a modern museum gives more details of both activities.

The third courtyard of the castle opens out to the east of the cathedral. Walk past the old Chapter House where you will find a heroic statue of St. George. The south side of the courtyard is dominated by the **Old Royal Palace** (Starý Královský Palác), home to Bohemian rulers from the 11th century until the Hapsburg takeover. Its somewhat modest façade conceals a fascinating building whose architectural style spans several centuries. The Romanesque early palace forms the foundations of the present structure. These were built during the last years of Přemyslid rule. Charles IV later enlarged the palace but it was Vladislav Jagiello in the late 1400s that created one of its finest extensions. He commissioned architect Benedict Ried to construct a large and ornate throne chamber. When it was completed in 1502 **Vladislav Hall** (Vladislavský sál) was the largest unsupported secular hall in the world, and today its wide expanse and roof supported by ribbed vaults is one of Prague's highlights. Vladislav was so pleased with it that he awarded Ried a knighthood. In the 17th century the hall was used as a meeting place but in earlier eras, royal tournaments were held with competitions in horsemanship. The horses were ridden up a wide gently sloping staircase to the hall which is now used by the many groups who tour the palace. Serious business went on in two rooms leading off the Vladislav Hall. **The Bohemian Chancellery** (Česká kancelář) was used for Bohemian government business. It was from this room that two governors and their clerks were defenestrated in 1618, precipitating the Thirty Years War. **Diet Hall** (Stará sněmovna) was the medieval parliament room. It was badly damaged in the fire of 1541 and rebuilt in the style of the time.

St. Georges Convent houses a variety of religious and royally commissioned art works.

From the Royal Palace walk east to another open square — St. George's (svatého Jiří náměstí). Here the buildings sport an ochre stucco façade. On the corner is the entrance to **St. Georges Basilica** (Bazilica svatého Jiří) said to be the oldest surviving church in Prague and founded in the early 9th century. The interior is austere in true Romanesque style — though it has been greatly restored over the centuries — with the scant remains of original ceiling frescoes. The basilica is the resting place of Queen Ludmilla, patron saint of Bohemia and other members of the Přemyslid dynasty. Towards the end of the 9th century the **Convent of St. George** (Klášter svatého Jiří) was established next to the basilica. The religious sanctuary was rebuilt many times over the centuries before finally being dissolved in 1782. Today it houses the Czech Republic's **National Gallery of Bohemian Art** (Sbírka starého českého umění), a treasuretrove of religious art and works commissioned by the ruling families during Bohemia's heyday — the Gothic period under Charles IV and the Baroque. Pride of place is given to a set of religious icons painted by Master Theodoric for the Chapel of the Holy Cross at Karlštejn Castle and dating from

1360. Other important Czech artists represented here are Petr Brandl and František Kupecký.

From the convent it is only a short walk to the eastern segment of the castle. **Golden Lane** (Zlatá ulička) nestles against the northern ramparts of the castle and comprises a wonderful collection of old cottages dating from the 16th century. They were first occupied by archers conscripted to defend the castle, and later by artisans — including goldsmiths, hence the name — and, some said, by alchemists. By the beginning of the 20th century it was an enclave for the poor. The writer Franz Kafka lived here in 1916 with his sister. Today the cottages have been restored to picture perfection and again house the products of artisans and pretty souvenir shops. Just watch your head as you enter · the lintels are extremely low!

Three attractions fill the walkway from Golden Lane to the east gate. **Lobkowitz Palace** (Lobkovický Palác), built in the aftermath of the 1541 fire, houses temporary exhibitions relating to monuments of the Czech past. These include documents and paintings. Across the street are **Black Tower,** a fledgling toy museum, and **Dalibor Tower** (Daliborka), which was used as a prison and named after its first prisoner, a young knight whose plight was also the inspiration for an opera by Czech composer Bedřich Smetena.

The steps below the tower lead down to the city below. In summer they play host to souvenir sellers who sit under colorful sun-shades. A lookout here offers wonderful panoramic views, and access to the gardens below the Royal Palace — resplendent after recent renovations.

The area of Hradčany, though dominated by the castle, has other attractions to explore. To the north of the fortifications themselves and across the deep moat — now a forested depression — is the **Belvedere Palace** (Belvedér palác), built

A modest summer home for royalty, Belvedere Palace provided a relaxing getaway for idle members of the Court.

in the 16th century by Ferdinand I and considered to be the only pure Italian Renaissance building north of the Alps. It was used as a summer house and the surrounding gardens must have been a welcomed area of relaxation for the members of the Royal court. They must have been much amused by the Singing Fountain, erected in 1568, whose bronze bowls resonate when hit by the jets of water. Unfortunately, much of the ornate sculpture work that originally decorated the garden was plundered by Swedish forces in 1648, but it makes a pleasant place to relax for today's visitors.

Walking west, away from the castle entrance at Hradčany Square, leads to another open square, Loretánské náměstí. Here you will find the beautifully ornate Baroque façade of the **Loreto** (Loreta), one of Bohemia's most important centers of

Christian pilgrimage. Its origins date to the Counter-Reformation in the 1620s, when, in order to increase faith in the Catholic religion, the Hapsburgs built replicas of the Sacred Santa Casa of Loreto in Italy all across their land. It was said that this original Santa Casa (Holy House and home of the Virgin Mary) had been carried by Holy men — or transported by angels — from Nazareth when Islam had overrun the Holy Land at the turn of the first millennium. However Prague's Santa Casa soon developed into far more than a simple shrine. By 1661 it was surrounded by ornate cloisters, which were then followed by Baroque decoration and a distinctive bell tower, created by Christoph and Kilian Ignaz Dientzenhofer (father and son), two of the most skilled architects of their time. Gifts poured in from around the kingdom and the treasury of the Loreta displays its amazing wealth, including a gold-plated and diamond-encrusted monstrance dating from 1699.

Across the square from the Loreta is the expansive façade of **Černín Palace** (Černínský palác), which occupies the entire western flank. Built for the Černíns, an influential diplomatic family in the 17th century, the palace was so huge — 150 m (500 ft) long — that it was said to have displeased Leopold I who felt that it rivalled the Royal Palace for splendor. Today it houses the Czech Foreign

Prague's rich religious history is evident at Loreto, in the Hradčany district.

Ministry and it was from one of these windows that Jan Masaryk fell — or was pushed — to his death in 1948 as the Communists rose to power.

North of the square is perhaps the prettiest, most unspoiled district in Prague. **Nový Svět** was formerly the poorest quarter in the castle district and as such was left undeveloped. Today it is home to many artists and has not yet been invaded by tourist shops or ticket sellers.

A couple of minutes west of Loreta Square, and overlooking the river and the city is **Strahov Monastery** (Strahovský klášter), founded in 1140. The complex was sited outside the protection of the city at the end of the road linking Bohemia to what is now Germany and it was the first such building for the Premonstratensian order. By devoting itself to research it continued to function until 1952 when it was dissolved by the Communist regime and the complex taken over for museums. Very little remains of the original Romanesque buildings though there are traces of Gothic and Renaissance features. The monastery is now almost totally Baroque in style, including two distinctive white towers.

Much of the monastery devotes itself to books as it houses the Czech **National Literature Memorial** (Památník

The miracle of Loreta.

One miracle attributed to the Loreta occurred during one of the plague epidemics in Prague. A mother had several children and each time one fell sick and died she paid a few coins to the sanctuary for the bells to be rung with a tune to the Virgin Mary. Eventually she was the only one left and when she fell ill and died there was no money to pay for the bells to be rung. Yet at the very moment she was laid to rest, the bells mysteriously rang out with the same hymn to the Virgin. The tune now plays every hour to accompany your tour.

*St. Nicholas Church (located in the Lesser Quarter)
holds a dominant position in the city's skyline.*

národního písemnictví). Part of the memorial, **Philosophical
Hall**, was built in the 1780s to house the collection of a
dissolved monastery in Moravia. Its walls are a feast of
polished timber bookcases filled with numerous valuable
editions of aged parchment bound with leather. The eye is
drawn up the cases to a highly decorated frescoed ceiling.
One religious building remains, the **Church of Our Lady**
(Kostel Panny Marie), with its rococo gilding and cherubic
ceiling paintings. Mozart is said to have played the organ in
the church in 1787.

MALÁ STRANA (LESSER QUARTER)

Lying directly below the castle, and reaching across to the
banks of the River Vtlava, is Malá Strana, the Lesser Quarter

or Little Quarter. The area was first settled in the 13th century when Otakar II invited German artisans to settle in Prague. Several ferocious fires destroyed the early town and although the street plan remains faithful to Otakar's original street plan, for the most part the buildings are later in date. Malá Strana became fashionable with wealthy Hapsburgs following the Counter-Reformation in the mid-17th century, and their money was invested in large mansions replete with Renaissance and Baroque details. Malá Strana is still a residential area, giving it an intimate atmosphere tangibly different to Staré Město just across the river (see page 44).

The heart of this quarter is **Lesser Quarter Square** (Malostranské náměstí) but the fine mansions, built with arcades over the cobbled sidewalks, have been somewhat overshadowed by the busy tram intersection here. In the center of

the square sits the **Church of St. Nicholas** (kostel svatého Mikuláše), one of the most prominent buildings on the Prague skyline and one of the architectural highlights of the city. The building is perhaps the crowning glory of the Dientzenhofer dynasty and completed just after the death of Kilian. Work began in the first years of the 18th century but the church was not finished until 1756. The

Rest your feet and ride the tram when exploring the Lesser Quarter.

distinctive 75 m- (245 ft-) high dome dominates the sur-rounding buildings but the interior of the church is a Baroque masterpiece with ceiling frescoes by Jan Lukáš Kracker fea-turing scenes from the life of St. Nicholas, and Franz Palko's *Celebration of the Holy Trinity* gracing the dome. Much of the flamboyant statuary is by Ignaz Platzer.

To the north of the square is the street of Letenská where you will see **St. Thomas Church** (kostel svatého Tomáše) abutting the road. Originally founded in 1257, it was one church that remained Catholic throughout the Hussite uprising and at the onset of the Counter-Revolution became a major focus of Catholic worship. In 1723 the church was badly damaged during a storm, and Kilian Ignaz Dientzen-hofer was commissioned to oversee its rebuilding. St. Thomas was once the church of a large monastery that had the sole right to brew beer within Prague. The brewery closed as recently as 1951, however the old medieval building is still utilized as the beer hall, **At St. Thomas's** (U svatého Tomáše), where you can enjoy traditional Czech hospitality. You will find the entrance a little way further down Letenská but be careful here as the road and tram-lines travel under arcades, making visibility difficult.

As you walk towards the Malostranská metro station you will pass the high walls of **Wallenstein Palace** (Valdštejnský

Finding your way around!

The street numbers of Prague can be confusing. Each building has two numbered plaques affixed to the wall. The blue plaque is the house or building number — the one you'll need if you are searching out an address. The red numbers indicate the order in which the buildings of a particular quarter were entered onto the municipal register; the lower the red number, the older the house.

palác). This extensive complex was the first Baroque palace in Prague and was built for Albrecht von Wallenstein, a favorite military commander of Ferdinand II. He started the palace in 1624 but soon fell victim to his own publicity and was killed on the king's orders in 1634 when he was found to be in secret talks with the enemy. The palace is now used for concerts and state occasions but you can enter the gardens for no cost and enjoy the formal lawns, fountains, and statuary. These are copies of works by famed sculptor Adriaen de Vries — the originals were stolen by Swedish forces during the Thirty Years War.

West of Lesser Quarter Square is **Nerudova**, a street leading ever upward towards the castle, and named after poet Jan Neruda, who once lived here. There are a number of fine buildings lining the route, each distinguished by an emblem as they were built before street numbers were introduced. Look out for "The Three Fiddles" at no. 12 or "The Green Lobster" at no. 43. Thun-Hohenstein Palace at no. 20 — its ornate entranceway framed by huge eagles — is now the Italian Embassy, and the Morzin Palace at no. 5 is a diplomatic base for Rumania.

South of Lesser Quarter Square, the houses are a little less grand but the streets are refreshingly quiet without the plethora of tourist shops found in other parts of the city. Walk down Karmelitska to find the **Church of Our Lady of Victories** (kostel Panny Marie Vítězné) on your right and named in honor of the victory at the Battle of White Mountain in 1620. Most visitors come to see the Holy Infant of Prague — a wax effigy said to be able to work miracles — which was brought from Spain in 1628.

From the church cross the street and head east to **Maltese Square** (Maltézské náměstí), which is filled with Baroque palaces, many of which are now embassy buildings. The square is named after the Knights of Malta who were given the nearby 12th century **Church of Our Lady Below the Chains** (kostel Panny Marie pod řetězem) as a gift by King Vlasislav. They built a large priory here that acted as protection for the Judith Bridge across the Vltava. The strange name of the church refers to the chain used to close the monastery gates. The church and surrounding priory buildings show vestiges of every era from Gothic to Baroque.

Nearby Grand Priory Square (Velkopřevorské náměstí) leads to the tiny Kampa Island. Here you will find the fading mural of John Lennon — now surrounded by graffiti added by visitors from around the world. This painting acted as focus for youth unrest in the final days of Communist rule. **Kampa Island** is separated from the Lesser Quarter by a branch of the river only 3 m (10 ft) wide. This was used to power water mills in days gone by. The island now boasts a pretty cobbled square and a large park.

Go down Karmelitská and, as it becomes Újezd, you will see the green parkland of **Petřín Hill** to your right. The vast open area stretching all across the hillside is in fact four different parks, but no one quibbles over the name. You can walk up the hill to-

A miniature Eiffel Tower — the old observation tower on Petřín Hill.

The ancient Charles Bridge is one of the most popular tourist attractions in Prague.

wards **Petřín Lookout** (Petřínská rozhledna) at the summit, but it is far less taxing to take the **funicular** (lanová dráha), which runs up the hill constantly throughout the day and evening. Once at the top you can stroll along the relatively shallow foot-paths to explore the attractions in the park which include the lookout tower — a mini Eiffel Tower — built for the Prague Industrial Exhibition in 1891, a children's playground, three churches, and the remnants of the Hunger Wall (Hladová zed') — a city wall built by Charles IV and said to be a community project to provide work and therefore food for the poor.

East of Lesser Quarter Square is **Mostecká** (Bridge Street). This short thoroughfare leads to the river. Lined with shops it leads the eye to one of the highlights of a visit to Prague — **Charles Bridge** (Karlův most).

Probably one of the most famous bridges in the world, the 520 m- (1,700 ft-) long, Charles Bridge was built across the Vltava in the mid-14th century following the loss of the previous Judith Bridge in a flood. Charles and his architect, Peter Parler, were determined to build a bridge that would last. But even they didn't imagine that it would last 600 years and counting.

The bridge was originally a very functional structure with little embellishment. At the Malá Strana end there were two towers. **Judith Tower** (dated c1190), the smaller of the two, is the only reminder of the Judith Bridge. **Lesser Quarter Bridge Tower** was built as a gateway to the town. Today it is open to the public and offers majestic city views. At the Old Town end of the Bridge is **Old Town Bridge Tower**, a masterpiece of Gothic architecture with a fine interior viewing room. This is also open to the public.

The numerous statues which now make the bridge unmistakable were mainly added in the early 18th century when the Italian fashion for bridge decoration spread throughout Europe. The exception to this is the **statue of St. John Nepomuk** (Jana Nepomuckého), which was erected in 1683 long before the saint was canonized and

St. John Nepomuk's statue has stood on Charles Bridge for over 300 years.

following his violent demise at the hands of King Wenceslas

IV. When his lifeless body was thrown from this bridge onlookers said that a holy spirit was seen rising from it and the story contributed to his revered status. Local people believe that the bronze relief depicting the final moments of the saint brings good luck, so rub the small upturned body to take some luck for yourself.

The bridge carried traffic until the 1950s — in fact it was the only way to cross the river until the mid-19th century — but it is now reserved only for foot passengers. In the evenings couples stroll arm-in-arm contemplating the water gently flowing downstream. In the daytime Charles Bridge can be one of the busiest parts of the city as groups march determinedly between tour venues. Numerous licensed artists set up stalls along its path to tempt you with watercolors or moody black-and-white photographs.

STARÉ MĚSTO (THE OLD TOWN)

While political power was invested in Hradčany, the Old Town — a cluster of streets on the opposite bank of the river — was the commercial heart of Prague. The city sat on important trading routes east/west from Krakow into Germany and north/south from Vienna to Warsaw. As the Bohemian *groschen* became one of the major currencies in Europe so the city began to take on a more grand appearance. Today it offers streets full of architectural delights from the medieval to the Baroque, but is also one of the busiest parts of the city. We'll start at the heart of the old town — Old Town Square (Staroměstské náměstí) — once the main marketplace for the city.

Old Town Square is arguably the center of Prague. It is a focus for tour groups, carriage rides, places of refreshment, and dates from 1390 and softens the façade of this immense Gothic edifice whose 15th-century towers rise to 80 m (260 ft) above the surrounding medieval streets. The church was a hot-bed of heresy from its earliest days and became the main Hussite place of worship as the reform movement grew in popularity during the 16th century. Following the Counter-Reformation it was handed back to the Catholic Church and has remained resolute to the present day.

The streets surrounding Old Town Square are a delight to explore. Almost every building has some highlight, from the tiniest detail such as a door knocker or carved lintel to a grand statement such as the superb Renaissance door at **House at the Two Bears** (Dům u Dvou Zlatých Medvědů) on Melantrichova. There's no better way to explore this part

An array of interesting architectural styles surround the central meeting place at the Old Town Square.

of town than on foot and much of the Old Town is traffic-free to allow you to stroll in safety.

East of Old Town Square to the river is probably most densely packed with fine mansions but is also one of the main areas for tourist shops and is often filled with people, which can spoil your ability to take in every detail. Next to Old Town Square is the much smaller **Malé náměstí**, decorated with a filigree fountain. On the east side, the highly decorated façade of **Rott House** (U Rotta) dominates the square. The paintings by acclaimed 19th-century Czech artist Mikoláš Aleš have recently been restored.

> Service can appear brusque, but a smile and a few words of Czech will change the atmosphere.

Karlova or **Charles Street** leads most directly to the Charles Bridge. Look for **Clam-Gallas Palace** (Clam-Gallasův palác), a magnificent Baroque building decorated with gargantuan statues by Matthia Bernard Braun. Just before you reach the river you will pass the high walls of the **Clementinum** (Klementinum), a former Jesuit college and the largest complex of buildings on this side of the river. The site began life as the Dominican monastery of St. Clement but was offered to the Jesuit brotherhood by Ferdinand I in 1556 to promote Catholic education. They commenced the **Church of the Holy Saviour** in 1593, whose domes now form one of the most recognizable outlines in the city. By the middle of the 17th century the Jesuits had a monopoly on education in the city as the Hussite faculty of the Carolinum (see page 56) was disbanded. The Clementinum expanded as the university grew resulting in a large part of the old town being demolished in 1653, though this process was not complete for another hundred years. When the Jesuits were dissolved by papal decree in 1773, the Clementinum became home to the library of the secular Charles University. Today it is the **National Library** and the churches are used as venues for concerts.

The approach to Charles Bridge is marked by the small **Knights of the Cross Square** (Křižovnické náměstí), decorated with a majestic statue of Charles IV erected here in 1848 on the 500th anniversary of the founding of Charles University. On the north side is the **Church of the Crusader Knights** dedicated to St. Franciscus Seraphicus (svatého Františka Serafinského). It is the one church that is only open for services. From here the bridge beckons but we will remain on this bank.

South of the bridge is a small outcrop with several buildings. Farthest away, with a wonderful view of the river, bridge, and castle beyond is **Smetena Museum** (Muzeum Bedřicha Smetany), which pays homage to one of the Czech Republic's most beloved composers and musicians.

A little way south of Karlova is **Bethlehem Square** (Betlémské náměstí) where you will find a reproduction of the 14th-century **Bethlehem Chapel** (Betlémská Kaple). It was here that Jan Hus began his historic campaign to reform the Catholic Church, which ended in his execution for heresy. One major form of protest was to conduct mass in Czech instead of Latin. Just around the corner from here, the remains of a small rotunda — in the process of refurbishment — dates from the 12th century.

The area north of Old Town Square has quite a different character from the rest of the Old Town. This is **Josefov**, once one of the most active and influential Jewish communities in Eastern Europe and still home to an orthodox community. To reach Josefov, walk down **Pařížská**, by the side of the Church of St. Nicholas. This street, as the name suggests, is reminiscent of a leafy Paris boulevard complete with fine boutiques.

The Old-New Synagogue holds an important place in Europe's Judaic history.

The Jewish community was founded in the latter years of the 11th century. Throughout the centuries the Jews were alternatively accepted and ostracized by the ruling dynasties. Certainly they were never allowed to expand beyond this small quarter. There was a devastating fire in 1689, and in the 1890s many buildings in the quarter were demolished to make way for new more sanitary housing, but several important buildings were saved. In the days leading to Nazi genocide of the Jews in WWII, the treasures of numerous synagogues in Bohemia were brought to Prague for safekeeping and in order that a museum might be founded to an extinct race after German victory. The collection is now managed by the Jewish Museum, which oversees several museums housed in the synagogues of Josefov.

   The Old-New Synagogue (Staronová Synagóga) is the oldest surviving synagogue in Europe. Built at the beginning of the 13th century it was named the New Synagogue but when a newer synagogue, now demolished, was built nearby was renamed Old-New. It is one of the finest medieval buildings in the city. The brick gables on the exterior were added in the 15th century. The main hall is reached through a small arched doorway featuring an elaborate carving of a vine; the twelve bunches of grapes depict the twelve tribes of Israel. The interior walls have traces of 13th-century frescoes and later inscriptions of sections of the psalms.

Next to the synagogue is the **Jewish Town Hall** (Židovská radnice), the seat of the Chief Rabbi. Its pink Baroque façade sports a fine tower and two clocks which tell the time in Hebrew and Roman numerals.

The entrance to a complex of two synagogues and the Jewish Cemetery lies on Široká. The ticket office here offers a rate for one or all the Jewish Museum attractions, or you can buy tickets at each separate venue. At this site, the **Pinkas Synagogue** (Pinkasova Synagóga) began life as a private family place of worship though it was later expanded to rival the Old-New Synagogue. Following the end of

Spend some time investigating the many features of Josefov, Prague's Jewish Quarter.

WWII, the names of all Czech victims of the Holocaust were inscribed on the walls of this synagogue; a stark and powerful tribute to those who lost their lives.

Travel through the outer courtyard of the synagogue to reach the **Old Jewish Cemetery** (Starý židovský hřbitov). This small area was once the only burial ground for Jews and as such each plot was used by several generations of the same family. It is thought that over 12,000 gravestones have been placed here, the earliest remaining dates from 1429; the most recent from 1787. The jumble of carved stones sits under the shade of mature elder trees adding a dappled light to this peaceful resting place.

The **Klausen Synagogue** (Klausová Synagóga) sits on the far side of the cemetery and was built on the ruins of a school or *klausen* in 1694. It displays artifacts relating to Jewish history and customs, including biographical information about the major figures of the Jewish community of Prague such as Rabbi Löw, who was suspected of working with the supernatural. His ornate tomb in the cemetery is always decorated with stones placed there by well-wishers.

The Jewish Museum is responsible for two other synagogues. Nearby **Maisel Synagogue** (Maiselova Synagóga) on Maiselova, which also began life as a private house of prayer — that of Mordachai Maisel who acted as banker to Emperor Rudolph II. The original structure was lost in the fire of 1689, but this ornate building replaced it, and it makes a fine backdrop to the collection of treasures it displays. Rare items of religious significance dating back to the Renaissance including liturgical silver, textiles and manuscripts can be viewed here.

Finally the most recent addition to the Jewish Museum is perhaps its *pièce de résistance*. The **Spanish Synagogue** (Spanělská Synagóga), a little way east on Vězexská, is newly renovated and its 1860s Moorish architectural style and wall decoration, reminiscent of the palace at Alhambra in southern Spain from which it got its name, are truly dazzling. The richness of the interior is in total contrast to the simplicity of the Old-New Synagogue.

On the outskirts of Josefov are three attractions which are not associated at all with the Jewish community. The **Museum of Decorative Arts** (Uměleckoprůmyslové museum) occupies a French style neo-Classical building whose rear overlooks the Old Jewish Cemetery. It is a showpiece for all types of decorative art, at which the

The Spanish Synagogue reflects the architectural style of the Moors.

Bohemians have consistently excelled. The museum holds one of the world's largest collections of antique glass with many fine domestic pieces. There are also displays relating to ceramics, tapestries, costumes and clocks.

Riverside of this museum is the large neo-Renaissance façade of the **Rudolfinum** (Dům umělců), one of the finest concert venues in the city and home to the Czech Philharmonic Orchestra. It acted as the seat of the Czech parliament immediately after independence in 1918.

Also on the banks of the Vltava but a little way north is **St. Agnes's Convent** (Klášter svaté Aneżky). The convent was

Come to the Rudolfinum for some of the finest symphonic music Prague has to offer.

founded in the first half of the 13th century by the Poor Clares, and at its prime was a large complex of several churches and cloisters before it fell into decay. Today the remaining buildings have been restored to house an exhibition of 19th century Czech painting and sculpture including works by the renowned Mánes family and Mikoláš Aleš. The convent also acts as a venue for concerts and temporary exhibitions.

East of Old Town Square, beyond the Church of Our Lady before Týn is a collection of narrow historic lanes with the pretty **Church of St. James** (Kostel svatého Jakuba), and a major thoroughfare, **Celetná**. Now a traffic-free walkway, it was once the major entry route to the city from the east. A stroll along Celetná reveals many fine houses, little alleyways, courtyards and deep cellars. Faint traces of Renaissance Prague can be seen amongst the flowery Baroque decoration. The **House of the Black Madonna** (dům U černé Matky boží) at number 34 looks little different to its neighbors yet dates from the early 20th century. The huge windows of this Cubist masterpiece reveal its original use as a department store. The statue on the façade after which the house is named is missing at present, but the interior is now the

Czech **Museum of Fine Arts** with a small but select collection of Cubist masterpieces.

At the eastern end of the street is **Powder Gate** (Prašná Brána), a tower dating from the end of the 13th century. It was one of a number of gates into the Old Town and marked a change from the previous defensive structure to a ceremonial entranceway. Originally it was linked to a palace called the Royal Court which was demolished at the beginning of the 20th century after laying derelict for a number of decades. In its place — almost as a phoenix rising from the ashes of Royal Court — is one of Prague's foremost Art Nouveau buildings, **Municipal House** (Obecní dům). The complex was planned

and built in the first decade of the 20th century to provide new exhibition space and, at the heart of the building, a modern auditorium. Municipal House was one of the first buildings in Prague to benefit from the now widespread renovation process, and the result has caused controversy in architectural circles. Its auditorium, **Smetena Hall**, is well established as one the major arts venues in the city and there is a fine Art Nouveau café on the first floor.

The Powder Gate is a reminder of the medieval portion of the city's history.

From Powder Gate, come back into the Old Town and one street south of Celetná is Železná — also traffic free. In the middle of the street you'll immediately see the wrought iron decoration of **Estates Theatre** (Stavovské divadlo) ahead. Built in the 1780s, the lines are some of the finest examples of neo-Classical architecture in the city and it formed the centerpiece of social activity in Prague when it opened. On 29th October 1878, Mozart conducted the premier performance of his new opera *Don Giovanni* here in front of a rapturous audience. The theater rekindled its relationship with Mozart when it was used as a set for the film *Amadeus,* directed by Czech Miloš Forman.

Next to the theater lie the remains of the first university of Prague. The **Carolinum** (Karolinum) was founded by Charles IV and named after him. Jan Hus served as rector here and the campus became a hot-bed of Hussite activity. After the victory of the Counter-Reformation it was handed over to the Catholic Jesuits and merged with their Clementinum complex near the river. Much of what remains here dates from the 18th century but look for the beautiful oriel window overhanging the street between the Carolinum and Estates Theatre.

The Royal Route

Powder Gate marked the start of the so-called Royal Route, the route which the coronation processions of the Bohemian kings and queens took through the city, and which linked Royal Court Palace and Hradčany Castle across the river.

Carriages would travel down Celetná, through the Old Town Square and along Karlova before heading across Charles Bridge. Once in Malá Strana they would travel along Mosteká into Lesser Quarter Square before making their way via Nerudova to St. Vitus Cathedral in the castle where the new monarch would be crowned.

NOVÉ MĚSTO
(THE NEW TOWN)

Charles IV gave the go-ahead for the building of the New Town in 1348 when overcrowding in the Old Town was becoming an acute problem. Although much of the first stage of building has been swept away in subsequent redevelopment, the New Town has many important attractions and is also a focus for hotels and entertainment — in the form of theaters, nightclubs, and cinemas.

The image of St. Wenceslas on horseback stands sentinel over the square.

Na příkopě is the street that was the traditional dividing line between the Old Town and the New Town. It was built over the old moat, the defensive structure around the Old Town — the remains of the bridge that spanned the moat can be seen at Můstek metro station nearby — and it links to the Powder Gate at its eastern end. Today it is traffic free and lined with modern stores and offices of the two major tourist information companies, Čedok at number 18 and Prague Information Service (PIS) at number 20.

The southern end of Na příkopě meets **Wenceslas Square** (Václavské náměstí), the symbolic heart of modern Prague for independent Czechoslovakia and the Czech Republic. The scale of the square is impressive. It's more of a boulevard than a plaza and puts one in mind of the Champs-Elysées in Paris at first glance. Huge crowds gathered here in

times of great joy and sorrow, most recently in 1968 to protest the arrival of Russian troops, and in 1989 to welcome the fall of communism. From Na příkopě there is a slight uphill slope, which leads the eye to the impressive vista at its southeastern end. However, though there are some fine buildings here, Wenceslas Square has suffered since the "Velvet Revolution" and now displays some of the tackiest tourist development in Prague.

Waiting in line is expected here.

Pride of place still goes to the **Café Evropa,** an Art Nouveau gem with a terrace where you can watch the world stroll by. The hotel to which it belongs was once the toast of the city and retains a certain faded splendor. Look also for Weil House with Art Nouveau decoration by Mikuláš Aleš.

At the top of the square sits the **St. Wenceslas Monument**, a statue of the saint astride a noble steed. Below the great man are life-sized statues of the other patron saints of the former Czechoslovakia. A work by Josef Myslbek, it is perhaps one of the best-known images of the city and was erected in 1912. Just below this immense monument is another simpler yet very poignant monument commemorating those **Czechs who were victims of the Communist regime**. In 1969 two young Czechs set themselves alight in the square, in protest of the Russian intervention to end the "Prague Spring." This memorial uses their fate as a focus for others who suffered or died.

At the head of Wenceslas Square is the **National Museum** (Národní Muzeum). Created at a time of rising national consciousness in the late 1890s its neo-Renaissance styling makes a confident statement with a beautifully decorated exterior and grand interior; however, the exhibits don't do the setting jus-

Not Prague's most progressive museum, the National Museum holds a stately position in St. Wenceslas Square.

The National Theater building, near the river Vltava, is a striking blend of old and new architectural styles.

tice — though they are in keeping with the age of discovery that was taking place at the time. There are collections relating to mineralogy, archaeology, and anthropology.

North of the museum along Wilsonova — always busy with traffic — is the Czech **State Opera** (Státní Opera), formerly called the Smetena Theatre and neo-Classical in design. Beyond this is the main railway station built in Art Nouveau style though now careworn.

From Wenceslas Square, the bulk of the New Town lies in a southwesterly direction, between the busy Sokolská and the river. We'll start at the northwestern end of Wenceslas Square and travel towards the Vltava. **Jungmannova** is now one of the prime shopping areas of the city with department stores, up-market galleries and exclusive boutiques.

On the northern side of Jungmannova Square (Jungmannovo náměstí) is the **Church of Our Lady of the Snows** (kostel Panny Marie Sněžné); look for a curious cubist lamppost just outside the entrance. Founded by Charles IV to mark his coronation in 1347, it was intended to become a triple-isled structure, but work was interrupted by the Hussite uprising. What remains today is simply the chancel of the original plan and in standing alone it seems completely out of scale to its floor area.

Follow Národni in the direction of the river to find the **National Theatre** (Národní divadlo) and New National Theatre. The first, an impressive building that adds grace to the riverfront vista, was built as the result of a groundswell of demand for an independent theater in the middle of the 19th century. In 1881, just before the theater was due to open, it was totally destroyed by an accidental fire, however such was the level of national pride at the time that within weeks the money had been raised to rebuild. Many of the finest Czech artists of their day were commissioned to work

---

The assassination of Reinhard Heydrich

On 17 May 1942 three men parachuted into Czechoslovakia from England and assassinated Reinhard Heydrich, the Nazi governor of Czechoslovakia, by throwing a bomb into his car as he made his way to his office in Prague Castle.

The incident enraged Hitler, who ordered an immediate and terrible reprisal on the Czech people. On 10 June that year, the population of the village of Ledice, some 25 km (16 miles) from Prague, was rounded up. The men were shot dead and the women and children sent to concentration camps before the buildings were razed to the ground.

Today the site of the former village is a memorial to those innocent victims who lost their lives.

---

on the theater, which was renovated in the 1980s when Karel Prager was commissioned to design the New National Theatre to expand the complex. It is one of the most striking examples of modern architecture in the city, presenting three cube buildings with exterior façades of glass bricks, and it acts as a permanent home to the National Theatre Company and Lanterna Majika.

Once at the river you'll see the Slovanský Ostrov island to your left. The island didn't exist until the early 1700s and following work to shore up the banks it became the center of social life in the city. The distinctive Renaissance tower here is linked to the Bauhaus, Manés Gallery — headquarters of the Manés group of artists who take their name from the 19th century Czech artistic dynasty. It has a changing program of *avant-garde* exhibitions.

Further south down the Masaryk riverside boulevard, on the corner of Resslova, is another fine example of modern architecture. The Tančící dům, or dancing building, was designed by American architect Frank Gehry in the early 1990s and has become known locally as the **Fred and Ginger Building.** A flowing glass and concrete tower (Ginger) seems held by the upright tower that is Fred, as if they were on the dance floor.

Walk down Resslova to find the **Church of St. Cyril and St. Methodius** (kostel svatého Cyrila a Metoděje). Methodius, regarded as the father of Czech Christianity, was ably accompanied by St. Cyril. Built in the Baroque period (c1730) this church was originally dedicated to St. Charles Borromeo and served retired priests. It closed in 1783 but in the 1930s was reopened under the auspices of the Czech Orthodox Church, hence the name change. The church became embroiled in one of the infamous acts of WWII in May 1942 when, after they had assassinated Reinhard Heydrich, the gunmen sought refuge in the crypt. When the church was surrounded by German soldiers the group decided to take their own lives rather than surrender. There is always a small memorial outside the church where bullet holes from the incident can still be seen. Inside the crypt are more photographs and artifacts relating to the individuals concerned.

The eastern end of Resslova meets **Charles Square** (Karlovo náměstí), probably the largest in the city. Laid out in the original city plan of 1348, it was originally the biggest market in Prague and was known as the Cattle Market. In the mid-19th century the square was transformed with the creation of a garden area, which today offers a place for local city dwellers to relax. The surrounding apartment blocks are not particularly exciting but **Faust House** (Faustův dům) has been preserved and recently refurbished. This site was a center of alchemy for many generations — in the 16th century it was home to Englishman Edward Kelley who was charged by Emperor Rudolf II with turning base metal into gold. The many secretive practices fostered its association with the Faust legend.

Walking north towards the Old Town you will find **New Town Hall** (Novoměstská radnice) at the end of Charles Square. Building commenced in 1348, and it was the site of the first

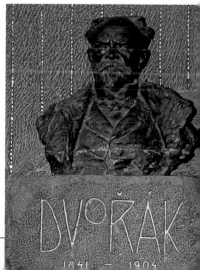

Antonín Dvořák is one of Prague's most celebrated musical contributors.

DVOŘÁK

1841 — 1904

defenestration of Prague in 1419 that precipitated the Hussite War. Several additions were added in the 16th and 18th centuries but the 15th century tower is now the crowning glory of the building.

Before strolling back into the main part of the town, take a detour to **U Fleků** on Křemencová. This is probably Prague's most authentic beer hall and has been open since 1499. It only serves the strong dark beer that it brews on premises — it is the smallest brewery in the city — and patrons sit at long tables in traditional wooden panelled drinking rooms. You can also try Czech food and enjoy a nightly cabaret act.

For two of New Town's attractions it would be easier to hop on the metro rather than walk. Both can be reached from I. P. Pavlova metro station in a couple of minutes. **The Chalice Restaurant** (U Kalicha) on Na bojišti is famed as the favorite drinking hall of Jaroslav Hašek, the writer whose most celebrated character, *The Good Soldier Švejk,* has become a national hero in the Czech Republic.

Nearby is the fine Baroque mansion known as Villa Amerika. Designed by Kilian Ignaz Dienzenhofer it was originally used by the Michna family as a summer palace and was completed in 1720. Today it houses the **Dvořák Museum** (Muzeum Antonína Dvořáka) with memorabilia relating to one of the great Czech composers. There are live recitals during the summer, however recorded Dvořák compositions play when the musicians are not present.

OUTLYING AREAS

The outlying suburbs of Prague have a preponderance of dour modern apartment blocks to house the growing population. However there are a number of attractions that make a trip on the metro or tram worthwhile.

These beautifully detailed doors open to the church in Vyšehrad, named for both saints Peter and Paul.

Vyšehrad
(Vyšehrad metro station)

Vyšehrad (meaning high castle) has an important place in the Czech national psyche. Here on this rocky mound over looking the Vltava, the legendary Přemyslid princess Libuše foretold the founding of a great city on the banks of the river. She is said to have married a common man, and their children were the founders of the Czech nation. Unfortunately for the legends, archaeological activity can only date the settlement here to the 10th century, making it younger than Prague Castle.

The castle was built (c1085) by Přemyslid leader Vratislav II and his two successors, who sought to consolidate power within their growing kingdoms. Along with a castle, an abbey was built, and later a Romanesque basilica. Power was transferred to Prague Castle by the end of the 12th century, however Charles IV breathed new life into Vyšehrad with new fortifications and large mansions in homage to his mother, who was descended from the Přemyslid dynasty. During the Hussite uprising many of the fortifications were destroyed, to be rebuilt in the later 1600s — the walls we see today.

From the metro station, a short walk will lead through Baroque **Leopold Gate** (Leopoldova brána) and on to a simple stone church. This is **St. Martins Rotunda** (Rotunda svatého Martina), one of the oldest churches in Bohemia. Built in the 11th century it was never extended or replaced though it was restored in the late 1800s.

Make your way to the neo-Gothic **Church of Saints Peter and Paul** (Kostel svatého Petr a Pavel) built on the site of earlier places of worship. At this time, Vyšehrad mythical status as the birthplace of the Czech nation was gaining favor again with the growth of nationalism. It was decided that the cemetery here would become, in effect, a **national cemetery** for famed and worthy Czechs: a focus for national pride. The cemetery has some fine sculptures carved by masters of their art and amongst the luminaries resting here are composers Antonín Dvořák and Bedřich Smetena and poet Jan Neruda.

National Technical Museum (Národní Technické Muzeum)
(tram routes 1, 8, 25, 26)

This rather plain 1930s building hides a wealth of machinery relating to man's technical achievements. There are sections on astronomy, cinematography, and industry — illustrated by the recreation of a coal mine. However, the main focus of the museum is the huge collection in the "history of transport" section. Here you can find cars, trains, and airplanes dating from their very earliest days of development. Czech-made examples feature prominently.

The Museum of Modern and Contemporary Art
(tram routes 5, 17, 53)

Founded in 1995 in the Trades Fair Palace (Veletržní palác), a masterpiece of 1920s architecture, the National Gallery's modern art collection showcases work from the 19th and 20th centuries. The redesigned interior of the palace offers a contemporary viewing environment very suited to its collection. Though the works strongly feature Czech artists such as Mikoláš Aleš — who was at the forefront of the "generation of the National Theatre" group — its strength for foreign visitors may well be in its French collection.

The collection was brought together with the precise aim of representing the major transitions of French art. Many of the works on show were bought by the Czech State in the 1920s. Each major modern school or artist is represented here, from the Barbizon School to influential Cubist works by Picasso and Braque. The museum also has works by Gauguin, Cézanne, and Delacroix, along with a range of Impressionist canvasses.

Prague was influential in art, photography, and architecture in the early 20th century and the gallery offers an interesting exposition on the important individuals of each genre.

The Exhibition Ground and Stromovka Park (Výstaviště a Stromovka)
(tram route 5, 17, 53)

Stramovka was for many centuries a royal hunting ground before being designated a public park in 1804. Today, its woodland and lakes make a pleasant alternative to the sometimes hot

and dusty city streets. The Exhibition Ground was chosen as the location of the Jubilee of 1891 and its large buildings still host regular exhibitions, concerts, and other events. A huge summer funfair is also a draw for both visitors with children and Prague's youngsters.

Mozart Museum (Bertramka)
(tram route 4, 7, 9, 34, 58)

Bertramka was the villa where Mozart stayed on numerous occasions during his visits to Prague. It sits on a wooded lot, which would have been some way from the hubbub of the city at that time. Mozart composed elements of the opera Don

Close to the city center, Letná park is home to this particularly ornate structure.

Giovanni during a visit in 1787 only hours before he debuted the work at the Estates Theatre. The small museum displays letters and scores in the hand of the great man, along with a number of musical instruments. In summer there are recitals in the courtyard, which adds an extra dimension to your visit.

Letná Park

Set on the banks of the Vltava opposite the Jewish Quarter, Letná Park is another open space within easy reach of the city. Not as well managed as the Petřín area it is nevertheless worth a visit because its southern edge offers superb views down the river and across the Old Town. Visitors are also drawn to a strange modern sculpture that sits on a concrete plinth over-looking the Vltava. The constantly swaying arm of a giant metronome was installed here after the "Velvet Revolution," on the site of a huge statue of Stalin that was blown up after the Russian dictator's death. The metronome also has its critics, but it's certainly a talking point.

Troja Palace
(Trojský Zámek)
(Holešovice metro station then bus route 112)

Set north of the city on the banks on the Vltava, Troja Palace was built as a summer home for the Sternberg family and it was the place to be when it was completed in the 1780s. Designed in classic Italianate style, the interior was decorated with fantastic frescoes — particularly impressive in the Grand Hall. The images here feature Hapsburg Emperors Rudolph I and Leopold I. The gardens sloping down to the river were in French style — a new innovation in Prague. Both house and garden were restored in the 1990s in line with the original designs, and the palace now houses the collection of the Prague Municipal Art Gallery with works from the finest Czech artists of the 19th century.

Prague Zoo (Zoologická zahrada)
(Holešovice metro station then bus route 112)

Neighbor of the Troja Palace, the zoo was founded on a large hillside lot. A chair-lift carries visitors to the upper displays. Over 500 species are on show here, a number of which are particularly rare. Prague acts as a breeding and research center for the preservation of these endangered animals, and the zoo is renowned for its successful breeding of the Przewalski horse, a miniature type that is now extinct in the wild.

EXCURSIONS

A day trip from Prague will open up much of the western section of the Czech Republic to you. There are numerous medieval towns as yet untouched by redevelopment or over-renovation, fine royal fortresses and various hunting lodges, along with hundreds of acres of the beautiful rolling Bohemian countryside.

For those who don't want to hire a car, there are several companies who offer a range of morning or day trips by bus.

The locations listed below will be included on their itineraries; it is simply a matter of which one to choose and your method of getting there.

Karlštejn Castle (hrad Karlštejn)

Charles IV transformed Prague into a sparkling capital city, and as Holy Roman Emperor, his own personal wealth was immense. Though Hradčany Castle was the center of court, Charles wanted somewhere secure to

The towering hrad Karlštejn dominates the village below.

keep his treasures, including the crown jewels and valuable Holy relics such as thorns from the crown of Christ and the tooth of John the Baptist. He commissioned the building of the Karlštejn Castle, 28 km (17 miles) southwest of Prague in 1348. Both Matthew of Arras and Peter Parler were involved in the process.

The site chosen couldn't have been better. Karlštejn is an imposing stronghold but it has also been cleverly hidden away in a narrow valley and would not have been visible to passing raiders. It could only be reached up a narrow valley making it easy to defend. Today it is probably the most popular trip from Prague and is invaded by thousands of visitors each week, however no tourist traffic is allowed up into the approaching valley so vehicles are left in the parking lot at the bottom of the hill, requiring a 15–20 minute walk to the castle entrance.

The first sight of the walls and turrets (from the village below) reveals Karlštejn to be a majestic sight. It fulfils everyone's idea of a medieval fortress, with high crenellated walls, interspersed with lookout towers. However it could not withstand the changes in modern warfare that preceded the Thirty Years War and suffered terrible damage at the hands of the Swedish forces and their field artillery. It wasn't until the 19th century that repair and renovation work was undertaken — some critics feel that this was overdone.

After entering the castle you will find yourself in **Burgrave's Courtyard** where your guided tour will begin. You will enter the Imperial Palace to view the **private apartments of the Emperor and Empress**, along with the **Great Hall**, used for entertainment and Royal court functions. The ornamentation in each room is splendid with fine panelling and Gothic ceiling detail. Exhibitions are devoted to the life of Charles and his influence on the society of Bohemia.

The **Marians Tower** or Tower of Our Lady above the palace has two important churches. The **Church of Our Lady** reveals some exceptional 14th century frescoes though it is said that many were lost in the 19th century renovations. One panel clearly shows Charles himself being handed several holy relics, including the holy thorns. A short corridor from the church leads to the tiny **St. Catherine's Chapel**. This was the emperor's private retreat where he would spend time in contemplation. It is encrusted with semi-precious stones and above the door is a portrait of Charles — dressed in a gold cloak and crown — with his second wife, Anna.

The castle **Keep** or Great Tower contained the most precious treasures. The **Chapel of the Holy Cross**, undoubtedly the highlight of the trip, is unfortunately now not open to the public. Earlier unregulated visits damaged the semi-precious stone decoration and the fragile paintings and frescoes. It was here that the Holy relics were kept, tended by a few chosen priests. The decoration in this, one of the most important holy places in the Christian Empire during the 14th century, is exquisite. The walls were covered with over 100 portraits of saints painted by Master Theodoric, the king's painter, in the 14th century — fortunately some have been removed and can be viewed at St. Georges Convent at Hradčany. The ceiling is awash with gold leaf.

Kutná Hora

Kutná Hora was the second most important town in Bohemia in medieval times. A healthy seam of silver found nearby fostered its rise in status — and helped to make

Bohemia one of the richest states in the world. However when the silver ran out in the 16th century, the city was left in a time warp. There are numerous protected buildings in the center of town and an increasing number of visitors are coming to enjoy its unspoiled character. The atmosphere is relaxed and genteel, and there are several places to enjoy a relaxed lunch.

The center of the old town used to be the Royal Mint or **Italian Court**, named because of the number of Italian artisans employed here. They were considered the most skilled at the art of coin design, which the silver mined here was most often used to create. Money funded building and development, and of course filled the coffers of the royal treasury back in Prague. The building was completed in 1300 and was designed with fortified walls and an internal courtyard. In addition to protecting the precious metal the court was also a royal palace used when the king came to oversee his money-making activities. Until recently the building played host to the Town Hall but now houses a small museum.

Nearby you'll find the mining museum housed in **Hrádek**, a partly Gothic structure. In the garden is the entrance to the medieval excavations and you can travel almost 50 m (55 yards) along the tunnels.

From Hrádek, walk up the hill along Barborská, with its ornate statuary and views left across the Bohemian countryside. To your right is the long elegant façade of the Jesuits seminary, the largest seminary outside Prague. Directly ahead is the jewel in Kutná Hora's crown, the magnificent **Cathedral of St. Barbara** (chrám svaté Barbory). Begun in the 14th century from designs by Jan Parler, son of Peter, it was almost complete by the 16th century. The structure represents one of the finest and most

dramatic examples of the Gothic style. However, the final plans for the church had to be altered due to funding problems and changes of architect and some elements date from as late as the 19th century.

The exterior features a tall main chancel supported by numerous flying buttresses. Three steeples shaped almost like the roofs of Bedouin tents rise above the buttresses. The ornate interior has Parler's trademark vaulting in the chancel and nave. A chapel dedicated to Jan Smíšek, Administrator of the Royal Mines, who was buried here in 1512, has fresco wall decorations featuring the mining and minting activities so important to the life and the economic well-being of the town. The cathedral was used as a set during filming of *Les Misérables,* when it took the place of Notre Dame Cathedral in Paris.

Karlovy Vary

Throughout the 18th and 19th centuries Bohemia was one of the most visited destinations in the world. Karlovy Vary 130 km (80 miles) west of Prague, and its sister town Marienbad, were an important element in its popularity. Both are spa towns and their waters are said to have therapeutic qualities.

It is said that Charles IV found the water source while out on a hunting trip in the forests here. He was chasing a deer, which in desperation jumped from a precipice into one of the hot pools. The town was christened **Karlsbad** in his honor — Karlovy Vary being the Czech equivalent of the Germanic title.

The Hapsburg court came to relax here and the newly rich joined them. Karlsbad was the ultimate high-class resort of

One cannot miss the façade of the church of St. Barbara — location set for the film **Les Misérables.**

Escape to the spa town of Karlovy Vary — a relaxing getaway from the city.

its time, with every modern convenience for its patrons. They included Czar Peter the Great, and musicians Bach, Brahms, and Grieg. Even philosophers such as Marx felt the need to tend to the body in addition to the mind. Karlsbad's visitors were often prescribed spa treatments by their doctors, and many came to escape the pollution of the newly industrialized cities.

Today there are 12 hot springs in the area. The best known is Vřídlo or "the bubbly one," and people gather to take the waters, though the fashionable and the glitterati have now turned their backs on the town. A stroll around the traffic-free streets reveals a few architectural gems and a pretty riverside promenade. You can also sit and relax in the elaborate wrought iron colonnades. The town has a robust arts program — another legacy of its up-market history — with an important film festival, theater performances, and concerts. It still aims to provide relaxed high quality vacations for those with taste and money. Fortunes have been lost at its casinos, and golf courses provide a round for those who just can't keep away from the greens.

Karlovy Vary is also a center of porcelain and glass production, and the only place in the world to make the aperitif *Becherovka* — locals call this alcoholic herb concoction "the 13th curative spring."

Marianbad, now **Mariánské Lázně**, lies in dense forest south of Karlovy Vary. There are well over 100 springs here and an array of 19th-century baths and sanatoria where you can fully enjoy the waters. Just as at Karlovy Vary, a range of summer concerts and shows take your mind off the taste of the water — slightly sulphurous — and take you back to the elegant days of the Austro-Hungarian Empire.

České Budějovice

One hundred and forty kilometers (90 miles) south of Prague is the beautiful 13th century settlement of České Budějovice. A trip here will fill a whole day and will allow you to enjoy the undulating farmland and forest that blankets southern Bohemia. The town was said to have been founded by Otakar II and its medieval square, reputedly the largest of its type in the world, is lined with beautiful Renaissance and Baroque houses. Czech poet Jan Neruda described it as "the Florence of Bohemia." Where Prague's houses now shine with new paintwork and refurbished statuary, the buildings here still have a patina of age. Being able to wander in relative solitude adds an extra dimension to the atmosphere. Look for highlights such as the **Dominican Monastery** founded in 1265, and the town's former arsenal built in 1530. Beer has been brewed here since the 16th century — the town gives its name to the famous Budvar or Budweis beer. If you want to enjoy a cool refreshing glass, visit Masné Krámy. Built in the 16th century as the town's meat market, it is now the most popular beer hall in town.

From the top of the **Black Tower** (Černá věž) in the town it is possible to catch a glimpse of **Hluboká Castle** nearby. This 19th century fortress is unique in Bohemia and has the outer appearance of a cake decorated with white icing. There has been a castle here since the 12th century and in the 16th century the Swartzenberg family took control. It was family member Johann Adolf who made the changes that we see today. He was inspired by the fashion for English gardens and so created one here in the Bohemian countryside. The interior of the house displays a collection of weaponry and some fine Flemish tapestries. You can also view the family's collection of Bohemian art — including many medieval religious works — in the converted stable block.

South of České Budějovice, the small town of **Český Krumlov**, with the second largest castle in the whole Czech Republic, has been designated one of the UNESCO World Heritage Sites.

Konopiště Castle (hrad Konopiště)

Archduke Franz Ferdinand was heir to the Austro-Hungarian throne in the early years of the 20th century but he was unpopular with his family for making a love match with a commoner.

The couple made their home far away from the royal court in Vienna at Konopiště, which the archduke purchased in 1887. Here they and their children enjoyed an idyllic life, however their happiness was cut short when in 1914 the archduke and his wife were assassinated in Sarajevo, precipitating the bloodbath of WWI. The castle here is worth a visit, as it reveals much about the life of this extraordinary couple.

Highlights

With so many beautiful buildings and important museum collections it is difficult to distill the attractions of Prague into just a few highlights, however we have created a list of the major must-see places to help you to plan your itinerary.

All museums of the Czech National Gallery are open from Tue–Sun 10am–6pm.

Sternberg Palace *Hradčanské náměstí 15; Tel. 20 51 46 34.* National gallery of European art. Open national gallery hours. Admission fee. (see page 26)

Royal Palace *Hradčany; Tel. 24 37 33 68.* Palace of the Bohemian kings and queens. Open Tue–Sun, Apr–Sep 9am–5pm, Oct–Mar 10am–4pm. Last admission one hour before closing. Admission fee. (see page 31)

St Vitus Cathedral *Hradčany; no phone.* The major Catholic place of worship in Prague, tombs of several important historical figures. Open daily Apr–Oct 9am–5pm, Nov–Mar 9am–4pm. Admission fee to crypt and chancel. (see page 28)

St George's Basilica *Hradčany; No phone.* Romanesque basilica with tombs of Přemyslid rulers. Open Tue–Sun Apr–Oct 9am–6pm, Nov–Mar 9am–5pm. Admission fee. (see page 32)

St George's Convent *Hradčany; Tel. 53 52 40.* Czech national gallery of Bohemian art — from the Gothic Renaissance and Baroque periods. Open national gallery hours. Admission fee. (see page 32)

Loreta *Loretánské náměstí; Tel. 32 10 51.* Place of Catholic pilgrimage with copy of the Santa Casa (the Virgin Mary's home) at its heart. Open Tue–Sun 9am–12:15pm, 1pm–4:30pm. Admission fee. (see page 34)

Strahov Monastery *Strahovská; Tel. 57 32 08 28.* Old monastery now housing the National Literature Memorial, with library halls and the Church of Our Lady. Open Tue–Sun

9am–noon, 1pm–5pm. Last admission 30 minutes before closing. Admission fee. (see page 36)

Church of St Nicholas *Staroměstské náměstí; Tel. 53 69 83.* Fine Baroque church with highly ornate interior by Christoph and Kilian Dientzenhofer. Open daily 9am–5pm. Admission fee. (see page 38)

Charles Bridge *No phone.* 600-year-old stone bridge on the River Vltava linking the two sides of Prague. No admission fee. (see page 42)

Old Town Hall *Staroměstské náměstí 1; Tel. 24 22 84 56.* City hall of the Old Town dating partly from the mid-14th century. Tower offers views over the city. Open Tue–Sun Apr–Oct 9am–6pm, Nov–Mar 9am–5pm. Admission fee. (see page 45)

New-Old Synagogue *Corner of Pařížská and Červená; No phone.* The oldest remaining synagogue in Europe. Open Sun–Thu 9am–5pm, Fri 9am–3pm. Admission fee. (see page 50)

Old Jewish Cemetery *Široká 3; Tel. State Jewish Museum 24 81 00 99.* Cemetery of the Jewish Community c1500–1800. Open Apr–Oct Sun–Fri 9.30am–5.30pm, Nov–Mar Sun–Fri 9.30am–4.30pm. Admission fee. (see page 52)

Spanish Synagogue *Vězeňská 1; Tel. State Jewish Museum 24 81 00 99.* Highly decorated 19th century synagogue. Open Apr–Oct Sun–Fri 9.30am–5.30pm, Nov–Mar Sun–Fri 9.30am–4.30pm. Admission fee. (see page 52)

National Technical Museum *Kostelni 42; Tel. 37 36 51.* Large collections of technical machinery covering transport, photography, cinematography, and astrology. Open Tue–Sun 9am–5pm. Admission fee. (see page 66)

Museum of Modern and Contemporary Art *Veletržní palác, Dukelských hrdinů 47; Tel. 24 30 13 08.* Collection of the masters of modern art. Open national gallery hours. Admission fee. (see page 67)

WHAT TO DO

ENTERTAINMENT

Prague is well-equipped with things to do, even after the museums and galleries have closed. You can avail yourself of the most high-brow forms of entertainment or enjoy mass-market fun. This is one city where there genuinely is something for everybody. Here are the main options; the choice, of course, is yours.

City Tours: Prague is a city suited to tours, with a wealth of pretty views, historic buildings, religious icons, and famous people — all of which can form a theme. There are a plethora of walking tours to choose from. Some cover the general history of the city, others specialize in particular aspects of Prague such as the history of the Jewish community, Baroque Prague, or Composers' Prague. You can join a group or book your own personal guide. Registered guides are highly knowledgeable about their city and their enthusiasm is definitely infectious. Contact Čedok

The Estates Theatre — What's in a name?

The oldest theater in Prague, the Estates Theatre opened in 1783 and less than four years later premiered Mozart's opera *Don Giovanni*, which he conducted himself. The theater was originally named because it was owned by the Czech Estates, however in 1945 it was renamed the Tyl Theatre in honor of J.K. Tyl, a Czech playwright, whose work *Fidlovačka* premiered here. Words from the work later became the song "Where Is My Home," the Czech National anthem.

or Prague Information Services for details of registered guides (see page 128).

If walking doesn't appeal to you then you can be educated and ride at the same time. Horse-drawn carriage rides carry you at a gentle pace through the cobbled streets of the Old Town; or take a vintage car ride — open top if the weather permits. Both of these tours can be taken from the Old Town Square. Or try a bus tour that can whisk you to the major sites in a few hours. You can take a river cruise along the Vltava either during the day or in the evening. Candlelit dinners or jazz band accompaniment add extra interest. Boarding takes place on the Lesser Quarter side of the river just below Charles Bridge.

One company offering walking, bus, or river cruises is Prague Sightseeing Tours. This company is a member of the Association of Travel Agents and can be contacted at Klimentská 5, 110 15 Prague 1; Tel. 2 231 46 61; fax 2 231 80 17; web site <www.vol.cz/pst>

Musical and Theatrical Performances: The city has been a major venue of musical performances for at least 5 centuries. It saw the premiere of Mozart's *Don Giovanni,* and the Hapsburg court played host to numerous major composers during their careers. Large concert halls have been built during various eras of Prague's history and today they, along with a host of smaller venues, arrange concerts throughout the year. Major orchestras appear at venues such as the Rudolfinum (Tel. 2 24 89 33 52) or Smetena Hall at Municipal House (Tel. 2 22 00 21 00). Lesser known touring groups or smaller groups such as quartets play at the Clementinum or St. Nicholas Church, among many others.

Revelers march in a street parade, exhibiting their local pride by sporting traditional Czech costumes.

Classical performers are highly esteemed in Prague, and can frequently be heard in concert throughout the city.

Throughout the year major festivals concentrate on the work of particular composers or musical styles. Favored composers include Mozart, Vivaldi, Bach, and Verdi, though Czech heroes such as Dvořák and Smetena are not forgotten. Concerts are held at lunchtime and in the evening and you'll find ticket sellers in the Old Town Square, or head to the box office of the venue itself. You could see a different performance every day, and with tickets available at such good value, many people do just that.

The city is also home to Czech national theater, ballet, and opera companies, and regularly hosts touring groups. The National Theatre (Tel. 2 24 91 34 37) is a huge complex with several stages and is the base for the National Opera and Ballet companies. It also includes the Laterna Magika

(Tel. 2 24 91 41 29), one of the major theater groups of Europe, which is at the forefront of improvisational performance. This genre blends music, mime, ballet surrealism, and satire, and the resulting melange seems to transcend spoken language (judging by the many nationalities that flock to see it). Estates Theatre (Tel. 2 24 22 85 03) also plays host to several companies each season and the Prague State Opera (Tel. 26 53 53) holds major productions of opera, ballet, and dance.

Marionette performances take place at the National Marionette Theatre (Tel. 232 34 29), where you can see the puppets perform sophisticated dramatic plays as well as fun things. Whichever type of performance you want to see, you'll find full details of what's happening during your time in the city by taking a look at the Prague Post, which has up-to-date information in English.

Nightlife

If you have had your fill of highbrow performances, then Prague offers a plethora of bars and cafés where you can enjoy a few drinks with live rock, jazz, or folk music. There's really nowhere better to enjoy a glass of local beer than at one of the huge beer cellars with their roving accordion players, though on a warm summer evening, try to find a bar terrace with a view over the city and watch the swallows swooping over the rooftops as the sun sets. This really is one of the beautiful and romantic cities in the world, so take time to savor the atmosphere.

As evening turns to night, Prague has a lively scene of nightclubs. The most popular change regularly so follow the local crowds, however the most longstanding club — still extremely chic — is Radnost FX at Bělehradská 120, Prague 2; Tel. 25 69 98 (metro station I.P. Pavlova). This has the top

Bohemian crystal is a favorite souvenir, and can be purchased in shops citywide.

local and invitation international DJs, and a gay night once each week.

SHOPPING

The 1990s saw huge changes in shopping in the city. This is one area where Prague has broken away completely from the old communist past of limited goods in state-owned department stores. Today it is just as exciting as any other city in Europe with an array of quality goods, handicrafts, and traditional products to tempt you to part with your crowns.

There are many European and US high street names taking flagship stores on the main shopping thoroughfares. However, the streets of the Old Town are filled with small specialist shops where you can browse for hours.

Do remember to ask whether stores take credit cards. Although the ability to pay by credit card is widespread, it is by no means universal.

Where to shop

Most of the major tourist souvenir shops can be found along the "royal way" from Municipal House through the Old

Town Square, and Lesser Quarter Square across the river. Numerous stores selling crystal, porcelain, garnet jewelry, and crafts will allow you to compare price and quality as you stroll along. Western high street names have taken space around Wenceslas Square and along Na příkopě, where you will be shopping among young affluent Czechs eager to embrace the latest fashion available. The more up market streets are Pařížská and Jungmannova, where designer names from Europe mix with those at the forefront of the burgeoning Czech haute couture scene.

Markets offer a range of goods. There is a craft market next to the Old Town Hall where you can buy marionettes, wrought iron work made before your eyes, and the ubiquitous T-shirt. The daily street market on Havalská has some souvenir stalls but concentrates on fresh produce for the tables of local people.

Finally, Charles Bridge is perhaps one of the most romantic shopping venues in Europe. No one can resist buying a little something from one of the many stalls as they admire the amazing view.

Bring home a whimsical handmade puppet, certain to delight any child!

Vendors display their colorful produce at a stall in the traditional New Town street market.

What to Buy

The Czech Republic has been held in high esteem for the quality of several of its traditional products. Glasswear and porcelain are particularly renowned and examples of both are found in royal collections all across Europe. Bohemian Crystal is a particularly high quality brand name though factories are scattered throughout the country. Lead crystal ranges in lead content from 14% to 24% and it can be found in myriad shapes and patterns. Traditional decanters, vases, bowls, and glasses with patterns cut by hand make pretty souvenirs or presents, and costs represent a 50% savings on European prices.

Modern design in glasswear is also very much in evidence. These range from large sculptured display pieces to vases. Bunches of large glass flowers mimic the shape of fresh blooms.

The delicate features of Bohemian porcelain figurines have changed little for the last 200 years, and the flowing form of the figures is highly regarded among collectors. The best come from small factories around Karlovy Vary, but they can also be bought from stores in Prague. You could also purchase classic dinner sets in the cobalt blue "onion" design made at the Český Porcelán factory outside the town, which also has an outlet on site.

With so much architectural beauty surrounding you, it is not surprising that art is in good supply here. Many visitors enjoy having their own portrait drawn or painted by the artists on Charles Bridge. There are also numerous stalls selling watercolors or line drawings featuring the classic views of Prague. Moody black-and-white photographs offer yet another view of the city. Aside from the obvious visual remembrances of the city, Prague also has several galleries selling "serious" art by both established and up-and-coming artists.

You will also find many antiques dealers in the city with musical instruments being particularly prevalent. Being a major city of the Hapsburg Empire, Prague had many rich and well-traveled citizens that owned treasures from around the world. These collections, along with a rich legacy of Bohemian furniture and other artifacts, form the basis of the modern trade in antiques.

Garnets have been mined and polished in the Czech Republic for centuries, and the pretty semi-precious stones can be bought in jewelers across the city. Often they are set in gold and silver to create necklaces, bracelets, or rings.

Amber is also popular but much of it is imported from Russia — do watch out for fake amber: If you want to buy, go to a reputable dealer.

Handicrafts come in a variety of forms and are sold from enticing stores in historic houses or ancient cellars. Wooden toys make good presents for young children. Sets of building blocks you remember from your childhood sit side-by-side with pull-along animals, or farm vehicles. Ceramics are made in a variety of shapes and decorated with glazes of almost every hue. Particularly attractive are the natural glazes produced with earth pigments. You can also find ceramic miniatures of the buildings of historic Prague, which you can arrange as street scenes. Buy every building on Old Town Square to recreate it on your coffee table at home. Textiles are also good value with woollen blankets and throws in a range of sizes. Decorated eggs feature prominently in Easter celebrations in the Czech Republic and eggs are widely available as souvenirs. They are decorated with a batik process where wax is applied in a pattern followed by color, which attaches itself to the surface of the egg that is free of wax. The result is a pattern of extraordinary complexity, all the more amazing when you realize the fragility of the eggshell. The eggs come attached to colored ribbons so that you can hang them in your home. Marionettes make an unusual and interesting souvenir and come in a range of characters. The craft stalls of Josefov have examples decorated as Rabbis; in other parts of the city you'll find show business or cartoon characters. Finally basket-wear — still used extensively in country homes throughout the country — is available. Unfortunately, the largest and most beautiful items would be too big to carry onboard the aircraft for your return journey.

In a city that inspired Mozart and Beethoven, and where classical musical performances are still such an important part of your overall vacation experience, it should not be surprising that music is a readily available souvenir. Also, CDs are inexpensive and take up very little room in your suitcase. Most of the street performers that you hear will sell CDs of their performances, however you will find several stores in the city selling a huge range of classical music — both on CD, tape, and vinyl. The haunting lilts of Czech composers such as Smetena and Dvořák take their inspiration from the countryside around Prague. Enjoy the waltzes of Strauss or the syncopation of Copeland — the shops of Prague stock the work of just about any composer you can think of.

Bottles of the delicious Czech pilsner beer are rather heavy to take home, however try a bottle of the potent *Becherovka* liqueur. Plum brandy or *slivovice* is widely available along with brandy distilled from other fruits.

SPORTS

The city itself is not well-endowed with sporting opportunities though the surrounding Bohemian countryside is beginning to be developed, offering outdoor pursuits such as kayaking and horseback riding.

Spectator Sports

Sparta Praha is the leading football/soccer team in the Czech Republic and has been one of the leading European clubs for many years. They play from a stadium just abutting Letná Park (Tel. 2 20 57 03 23) and their season runs from September to April. Ice hockey is also popular and the main venue for this is at the Exhibition Ground (Tel. 2 24 23 21 85). Horse racing takes place every Sunday from April–

October at Velká Chuchle, Prague 5 (Tel. 2 54 30 91) with trotting in the spring and fall. The Czechs are naturally proud of the number of professional tennis players they have produced in recent decades. The National Tennis facility on Štvanice Island (Tel. 2 232 46 01) below the Hlávkův Bridge hosts Grand Prix tournaments. Details can be found at the information office.

Participation sports: Golf can be found at the Motol hotel and sports complex (Tel. 2 651 24 64) on the outskirts of the city and at the Exhibition Ground, or head out to Karlštejn (Tel. 0311/68 47 16) only 28 km (16 miles) away where you can see the course from the castle turrets. Large golf courses

Local people spend a relaxing afternoon fishing from an open boat beneath the Charles Bridge.

are available at the spa towns a couple of hours from Prague. The course at Mariánské Lázně (Tel. 0165/43 00) regularly hosts PGA tournaments, while Karlovy Vary (Tel. 017/333 11 01) has the oldest club in the Czech Republic, inaugurated in 1904.

Tennis can also be played at the complex on Štvanice Island (Tel. 2 232 46 01) below the Hlávkův most, which is the Czech national facility and one of the best in Europe. To book ahead, see the number listed above, or contact the Motol complex.

THINGS FOR CHILDREN

At first glance Prague seems to have little to offer children, with the accent on touring major churches, palaces, and galleries. However, there are a few fun activities that will keep children happy, and perhaps add a lighter note for parents too!

Transport offers a diversion. Take a horse-drawn carriage ride through the streets of the old town, or perhaps one of the open top vintage cars. Your child will love being the center of attention, and will be able to get a better view of what's happening from higher up. Boat trips on the Vltava are also fun — take some bread to feed the ducks and swans, Very few cities in the world have a tram system, so a simple and inexpensive tram ride will be a thrill.

With a little forethought, a theater performance can be stimulating and entrancing for children. The Lanterna Majika features dance, mime, and the use of lighting effects. It requires no language skills and concentrates on visual entertainment, which is ideal for young ones. The National Marionette Theatre (Tel. 232 34 29) performs shows for all ages, including a puppet version of the opera *Don Giovanni*.

Children will enjoy feeding the graceful swans at the banks of the river Vltava.

If your child enjoys a fun-fair (and who doesn't?) there is a large one during the summer months at the Prague exhibition ground.

Fun museums include the National Technical Museum with its displays of vintage vehicles and a reconstructed coal-mine. There is a noise "laboratory" where kids can have fun making sound with different instruments. This is one place where they can be as loud as they want.

Or try the National Museum with somewhat old-fashioned collections of tropical insects and animal bones. Children are always enthralled by giant bugs!

Who can resist a trip to the zoo? Prague has 500 species of animals on show and works actively in conjunction with zoos worldwide in the preservation of 50 different types of rare animals. Pride of place is taken by a rare species of horse, the przewalski, a miniature breed which can now only be seen in captivity.

Short lunch time concerts at venues all across town may be the perfect way of introducing children to classical music. Who knows — you may have a budding Mozart or Yo Yo Ma in the family.

Calendar of Events

In Prague, the calendar of arts and music is extremely busy with numerous performances each week. This is beyond the scope of this guide. The best source of up-to-date information on performances while you are in the city is the Prague Post. However, here are some of the major annual events that you can experience both in the city and surrounding towns to help you plan your trip.

1 January — spectacular New Year celebrations across the city.

May — Prague International Marathon (dates change each year)

12 May–4 June — Prague Spring Festival (Praské jaro). One of the world's foremost classical music festivals, with performances by celebrated musicians at major venues throughout the city.

June — Smetana National Opera Festival.

July — International Film Festival at Karlovy Vary. Originally a forum for films from Eastern Europe, now embracing worldwide productions.

Prague Harp Congress. An international harp festival.

July–August — Prague Verdi Festival. Displays of music and dance in traditional costume. Communities travel from throughout Bohemia and Moravia to venues in the city.

August — The Chopin Music Festival held at venues throughout Bohemia.

September — Prague Fall Festival. International music festival.

October — Bi-annual Prague Jazz Festival.

October–November — Musica Iudaica. An international festival of Jewish music held at synagogues and concert halls.

November–May — United Colors of Akropolis at Palác Akropolis. A series of concerts around the theme of musical innovation and experimentation.

December — Advent and pre-Christmas activities such as craft markets, carol concerts, and an open-air arts festival.

EATING OUT

Czech food offers the perfect antidote to the rigors of health food and *nouvelle cuisine*: honest, filling, often delicious dishes, based on the kind of recipes grandmother kept to herself. You will also find that prices are still relatively cheap, even after several increases in the last few years, and it is very easy to eat well for $10 per person. Since the "Velvet Revolution," Prague has become one of the busiest tourist cities in Europe, and international chefs and restaurateurs have been quick to take advantage of the new opportunities. There is a surprising amount of international cuisine available in the city from sushi to Indian curries. The following is a guideline of the kind of menu items you will find in Czech restaurants, to allow you to sample the local cuisine.

Where To Eat

Eating places, with which Prague is generously endowed, have until recently been state licensed, but this system is beginning to change as more new establishments open and more international ideas find a foothold in the country.

Apart from conventional restaurants (called *restaurace*), which may be exclusive or geared to a regional or foreign cuisine, the following options are worth seeking out:

Vinárny ("wine restaurants" — on signs you will see the word *Vinárna*), may have the same menus as ordinary restaurants, but they highlight the wine accompanying the food. The ambience is often intimate, and possibly historic or folkloric as well.

Pivnice or *hospody* (pubs or taverns) specialize in draught beer and a limited variety of traditional meat platters; the mood is likely to be jolly, with informal service.

*Eat like a native — visit At St. Thomas' beer hall in the
Lesser Quarter, and feel the pulse of Prague.*

Kavárny (cafés) are essentially for snacks and sweet pastries, though you may find some hot meals on the menu. On signs you will see the word *Kavárna*.

If you're in a rush and need a quick snack, there is now a wide range of cheap fast-food outlets and self-service bistros in the city center.

The atmosphere in Prague's eateries is often colorful or romantic, though the standard of service is variable. Most waiters will understand a few English phrases. Some speak good English, but if you learn a few words of Czech it will certainly be appreciated. Smoking is very popular in the Czech Republic so it may be difficult to escape the fumes — especially in pubs. Terrace cafés and restaurants help to alleviate the problem. If a restaurant becomes busy it is normal practice for you to share a table — many pubs have long communal tables that seat 10 or 12 people.

Do be aware of the extra charges that most eateries and pubs add on. A cover charge is universal and will be around 30 Kč per person. Some budget cafés will charge for condiments, and others leave pre-appetizers on the table without telling you that there is a charge. Pubs will often send waiters around with trays of short drinks — becharovka or slivovice (see below) — but these drinks will be added to your bill. These charges are minimal but sometimes tactics can be a little underhanded.

Keep the change
To be dobr?

Breakfast

Breakfast (*snídaně*) is served by hotels from about 6am to 10:30am. Depending on the establishment the meal can be as simple as bread, butter, and jam with coffee and tea, or as beautiful as you could wish. In the better hotels, a lavish hot and cold buffet is served, but this is often an extra and sometimes hefty charge. Another option is to eat out at one of the American-influenced diners.

Lunch and Dinner

During the working week most Czechs eat early — generally around 7pm — and head to bed early in preparation for the working day ahead. However restaurants in Prague will stay open until around 10 or 11pm. At weekends hours are longer as local people come out to enjoy their free time.

Most restaurants post a typewritten menu (*jídelní lístek*) near the door, giving you at least an idea of the prices. Nowadays, most cheap, medium-priced, and first-class

*Calorie counters beware — traditional Czech food is
hearty and filling, as is the local beer!*

restaurants tend to have menus in English and German as
well as Czech.

The menu is divided into categories such as these: *studená
jídla* (cold dishes), *polévky* (soups), *teplé předkrmy* (warm
starters, or appetizers), *ryby* (fish), *drůbež* (poultry), *hotová
jídla* (main courses), and, to finish, *moučníky* (desserts). A
growing number of establishments are offering set meals at
lunch and dinner, in addition to an à la carte range.

Try an appetizer of Prague ham (*Pražská šunka*), a succulent local specialty. It may be served in thin slices, garnished
with cucumber and horseradish; with cheese in miniature
sandwiches; or folded into horns and stuffed with cream or
cream cheese and horseradish.

Soup is a popular choice at both lunch (*oběd*) and dinner
(*večeře*). It may be a fairly light bouillon or, more likely, a

thick, wholesome soup of potatoes, vegetables, and perhaps a bit of meat. A dab of whipped cream may also be added. One of the heartiest traditional recipes is *bramborová polévka s houbami* (potato soup with mushrooms). This thick soup flavored with onion, lard, carrots, cabbage, parsley, and spices can be a meal in itself.

> **Leave small change as a tip in a beer hall.**

The hearty Czech cuisine is typically based around well-roasted pork or beef with thick gravy. This is supplemented with poultry, game, or fish dishes — derived from a tradition of seasonal hunting in the surrounding countryside. The generally heavy, savory food goes down best of all with cold Czech beer, a brew admired for centuries by gourmets everywhere.

Meat dishes form the main strength of Czech cuisine. Meat is always well cooked, be it roasted or broiled. Most popular dishes include succulent *Pražská hovězí pečeně* (Prague roast beef), a joint of beef stuffed with fried diced ham, peas, egg, onion, and spices. Also, look for *svíčková pečeně na smetaně*, tasty beef in a cream sauce.

Another gourmet adventure is *šunka po staročesku* (old Bohemian-style boiled ham), involving a sauce of plums, prunes, walnut kernels, and wine. For memories of the Austro-Hungarian Empire, you should sample some *guláš* (goulash), a meat stew flavored with paprika sauce, or *smažený řízek* ("Wienerschnitzel"), a breaded veal cutlet. Poultry and game are also popular in Prague and depending on the season you will find duck, goose, boar, and venison on the menu.

For accompaniment, pride of place goes to the dumpling. Either made from bread, *houskové knedlíky*, (relatively light) or potato, *bramborové knedlíky*, (heavier in texture) you will always find one or two sliced dumplings on your plate. Vegetables have always played a secondary role in traditional cuisine and often appear overcooked in stews and soups. In fact you will often see "stewed vegetables" on menus in English, which lets you know that they won't arrive *al dente*. Sauerkraut *(kyselé zelí)* is most commonly served. The cabbage — either red or white — is softened in animal fat, sugar, and a little wine.

Desserts are usually in the heavyweight category, with tasty dishes like *jablkový závin* (apple strudel), with a topping of whipped cream. A slightly more delicate variation, *jablka v županu* (apple baked in flaky pastry), uses whole apples stuffed with sugar, cinnamon, and raisins. *Švestkové knedlíky* (plum dumplings) are sprinkled

Seasonal fresh fruits and vegetables are featured in local restaurant cuisine.

with cheese curd and sugar, and then doused in melted butter. A great favorite is *palačinka*, ice cream or cream and fruit enveloped in a pancake. Or perhaps settle for *zmrzlina* (ice cream) or *kompot* (stewed fruit) — sometimes laced with fruit brandy.

Vegetarians

The presence of a large expatriate community has ensured the emergence of several vegetarian cafés and restaurants over the past few years. Consequently, many non-vegetarian restaurants now offer a range of options *bez masa* (without meat).

One of the best places for vegetarian food is the Palace Hotel Cafeteria (Panská 12), open from noon until 9pm. Although the cafeteria is self-service, the standard of food is consistently high, and it has the best salad bar in town, with the added advantage of being smoke-free.

Snacks

Prague is a great place for inexpensive between meal snacks or lunch on the move, whichever you prefer. You'll find them sold at street stands in the city. A *bramborák* is a savory potato pancake, served greasy but deliciously on a piece of paper. *Pečená klobása* (roasted sausage) rates a paper plate, a slice of rye bread, and a squirt of mild mustard, but no fork or knife. You can also get them hot-dog style with onions and mustard. *Smažený sýr* is a sort of vegetarian Wienerschnitzel, consisting of a slice of fried cheese. *Chlebíčky* or open sandwiches with a variety of toppings are also popular in snack bars. You may be offered them if you are invited to a Czech home.

The ubiquitous American-style fast-food outlets can be found, particularly along and around Wenceslas Square. Among young Czechs these are more popular than the traditional snack outlets. Delicious ice cream is sold everywhere, and makes a refreshing snack on hot summer afternoons.

Drinks

Prague offers a wonderful selection of places to drink—and very many of them will provide light meals as well. The architectural richness of the city ensures a range of superb settings, added to which the thriving café society of the early 20th century is now beginning to re-emerge.

Czech beers are famed throughout the world and their major brewing region around the city of Plzen has given the world the *pilsner* style of drink, which many other countries have copied. Of course, local people would say that no other beer tastes the same, because Plzen beer gets its distinctive flavor

> In a beer hall, take a seat and place a beer mat on the table to let the waiter know that you want a drink.

from the alkaline water and the excellence of a key ingredient, hops, that grows on vast wood-and-wire frames in the Bohemian countryside.

There are also many other well-regarded breweries in Prague and the smaller surrounding towns. Several Prague pubs brew their own light (*světle*) or dark (*tmavé*) blends, including U Fleků, which has been brewing since 1499. All Czech beer is tasty and refreshing but do keep in mind that it's probably stronger than the brews you're used to drinking at home.

Czech **wine** (*víno*) is almost unknown abroad, so you're bound to discover something new and pleasing without having to look very hard. Bohemia produces only a small proportion of the country's total wine output. Most comes from Moravia, which has more sunshine, producing sweeter grapes. White is *bílé* and red is *červené*.

A drink local to Karlovy Vary, *Becherovka* is made of herbs and served chilled as an aperitif, as is the powerful, sweetish *Stará myslivecká*. After-dinner drinks generally mean fruit brandies, especially *slivovice*, which is made from plums.

Non-alcoholic drinks include pure mineral water bottled at the spa towns of Karlovy Vary and Mariánské Lázné, fruit juices, and international brands of soft drinks. Turkish coffee and Italian-style espresso are also very popular.

To Help You Order...

Could we have a table?	**Máte prosím volný stůl?**
The bill, please.	**Zaplatím**.
I'd like ...	**Prosím ...**

beer	**pivo**	meat	**maso**
bread	**chleba**	the menu	**jídelní lístek**
butter	**máslo**	milk	**mléko**
cheese	**sýr**	mineral water	**minerálka**
coffee	**kávu**	salad	**salát**
dessert	**moučník**	sugar	**cukr**
egg	**vejce**	tea	**čaj**
ice cream	**zmrzlinu**	wine	**víno**

...and Read the Menu

bažant	pheasant	**knedlíky**	dumplings
brambory	potatoes	**králík**	rabbit
drůbež	poultry	**kuře**	chicken
fazole	beans	**květák**	cauliflower
houby	mushrooms	**kyselé zelí**	sauerkraut
hovězí	beef	**ledvinky**	kidneys
hrášek	peas	**pstruh**	trout
hrozny	grapes	**rajská jablka**	tomatoes
hrušky	pears	**rýže**	rice
husa	goose	**špenát**	spinach
jablka	apples	**srnčí**	venison
jahody	strawberries	**štika**	pike
játra	liver	**šunka**	ham
jazyk	tongue	**švestky**	plums
jehněčí	lamb	**telecí**	veal
kachna	duck	**telecí brzlík**	sweetbreads
kapr	carp	**vepřové**	pork
klobása	sausage	**zajíc**	hare

HANDY TRAVEL TIPS

An A–Z Summary of Practical Information

A

ACCOMMODATIONS

Hotels. Hotels in Prague are expensive in relation to the other costs of your trip. There are many large hotels and very few of the *olde worlde* family-run establishments that can be found in other cities. Most hotels dating from the communist era have very dour exteriors though there was a program of renovation during the 1990s and many have been totally updated to bring the facilities and interior decoration up to international standards and star ratings. A few "gems" of the Art Nouveau era have also been renovated to offer a feel of one of the city's heydays. Most hotels will now have facilities in all rooms. This is the case with all hotels in the recommended list except the Evropa. Access for disabled visitors is variable so do make enquiries directly with the hotel concerned if this is a requirement for you.

Prague becomes very crowded with visitors at peak times — June to September and around Christmas time — so it is important to make a booking in advance to guarantee the standard of accommodation that you want.

Hotels are generally priced per room per night and can be priced in a foreign currency — often Deutsch Marks. Room prices in smaller, cheaper hotels will include breakfast. Breakfast may be an extra cost at four and five star hotels. A 22% tax may be included along with a municipal tax. Always ask whether the room rate includes tax before you make a firm booking.

B&B. The number of private homes offering bed and breakfast type accommodations has grown dramatically in recent years but prices and facilities differ widely between establishments. Both Čedok and Prague Information Services (PIS) offices will be able to help you with this form of accommodation (see TOURIST INFORMATION, page 128). Always check the exact location and transport connections for your accommodations in addition to the facilities before you make a firm booking.

If you arrive in the city without accommodations, head to one of the tourist information offices listed below. If you arrive by train there is also an information office, A.V.E. (Tel. 24 22 32 21) which can also offer advice. You may be required to leave a deposit with the information office. Sometimes this is non-refundable so ask before you make a reservation.

I'd like a single room/
   double room.
	**Chtěl bych jednolůžkový
	   pokoj/dvoulůžkový pokoj.**

with bath/with shower	**s koupelnou/se sprchou**
What's the rate per day?	**Kolik stojí za den?**

AIRPORT

Prague-Ruzyné is situated 15 km (9 miles) to the northwest of the city. It has become increasingly busy as the number of people visiting the city skyrocketed during the 1990s. The airport is constantly being updated and has all the facilities expected in a major international airport. It is served by several major international airlines in addition to Czech Airlines (ČSA), including British Airways, Air Canada, KLM, and Lufthansa. Delta operates flights via Frankfurt and most other major American airlines fly to Europe for onward connections to Prague.

You can travel to the city center by a bus service run by ČSA, which departs from the Czech Airlines Center. The schedule is every 30 minutes — there is a timetable at the arrivals lounge — and the journey takes around 30 minutes and costs 50 Kč. Pay the driver as you get on board.

A cheaper but longer service, the no.119, travels to the Dejvická metro station from where you can reach the center of the city. Buy a ticket in the terminal for this service.

Taxis also operate from the airport. Ask at the information desk about fares, which are currently around 500 Kč. There have been a number of complaints about taxi drivers trying to overcharge in recent years, so always agree on a price with the driver before getting in the taxi.

Where do I get the bus to the city center?/to the airport?	**Odkud jede autobus do centra města?/na letiště?**
Porter!	**Nosič!**
Take these bags to the bus/taxi, please.	**Prosím, odneste tato zavazadla k autobusu/taxi.**

B

BUDGETING FOR YOUR TRIP

Once you have paid for travel and accommodations, living expenses in Prague offer exceptional values despite several price rises in recent years. Here are some sample prices to help you to plan your budget.

Travel to Prague: Scheduled flight from London-Prague £120-170; Scheduled airfares from the US are advertised around $1,500 though deals are available. Eurolines 60-day coach pass £219-283, 30 days £175-245.

Airport transfer: Public transport 30-50 Kč/taxi fare 500 Kč

Public transport tickets: Individual ticket 8 Kč for 15 minutes travel or four metro stops with no transfer. 12 Kč for one hour travel with transfer. Day pass 70 Kč. Three day pass 180 Kč.

Taxis: Prices are supposed to be 25 Kč then 17 Kč per kilometer with an additional charge of 4 Kč per minute at busy times. There are also extra charges for baggage and the prices rise by up to 300% at night. It may be wise to negotiate a price for the journey before you enter the taxi rather than rely on the meter.

Car hire: rental for a medium-sized car 3,500 Kč per day with unlimited mileage or 1,500 Kč with 11 Kč per kilometer.

Hotel: Mid-priced hotel per room per night 4,000 Kč-5,000 Kč.

Meals and drinks: Large glass of beer 80 Kč; 3 course dinner per person 500–800 Kč; soft drink 100 Kč.

Entertainment: Theater tickets 250–500 Kč with state company or international performances around 1200 Kč. Concert tickets are 300–500 Kč.

Tours: Walking tour of the city (3 hours) 300 Kč; coach tour to Karlštejn Castle (5 hours) 820 Kč; Vltava river cruise (2.5 hours) 720 Kč.

C

CAMPING

There is a large camp site on the banks of the Vltava near the Troja Palace and the Zoo, which is the nearest to the downtown area. It has space for caravans and tents with good, although not luxurious facilities. Autocamp Trojská, Trojská 157, Prague 7. Tel. 68 86 036. This is open from April to the end of October. The Prague Information Center has more comprehensive details of camp sites throughout the surrounding area.

CAR RENTAL/HIRE

If you plan to stay in the city rather than touring the countryside, a car may be more of a hindrance than a help. The city is compact, many streets are for pedestrians only, and the public transport system is well-organized and cheap. If you want to rent a vehicle, most of the major car rental companies operate in the Czech Republic. You can pick up your car at the airport or have it delivered to your hotel.

Prices are not particularly expensive by international standards, however pricing structures can be complicated. Always be clear about what is included in the price and what will be added as extras. Extras can include local tax (currently 5%), additional driver charge, mileage, airport delivery charge, and collision damage waiver. If possible get an overall final price, and make price comparisons with several companies. Booking before you reach Prague can be cheaper and simpler.

Prague

The daily rental charge for a medium-sized car (by European standards) is around 3,500 Kč per day with unlimited mileage or 1,500 Kč with 11 Kč per kilometer. Most companies will have special rates for weekend rentals.

Collision damage waiver is not compulsory but limits your liability in the case of accident. It adds around 250 Kč per day to the rental cost.

Drivers must be at least 21 years of age and have held a full license for one year.

Contact these companies at the following addresses while in Prague. Most staff members will speak good English.

Avis — at the airport; Tel. 35 36 24 20; In the city at Klimentská 46, Prague 1; Tel. 21 85 12 25; web site <www.avis.com>.

Hertz — at the airport; Tel. 20 11 43 40; In the city at Karlovo náměstí 28, Prague 2; Tel. 22 23 10 10; web site <www.hertz.com>.

Europcar — at the airport; Tel. 316 78 49. In the city at Pařížská 28, Prague 1; Tel. 24 81 12 90; web site <www.europcar.com>

Thrifty — at the airport; Tel. 20 11 43 70. In the city at Washingtonova 9, 110 00 Prague 1; Tel. 24 21 15 87; web site <www.thrifty.com>

I'd like to rent a car.	**Chtěl bych si půjčit auto.**
large/small	**velké/malé**
for one day/a week	**na jeden den/týden**
Please include full insurance.	**Prosím, započítejte plné pojištění.**

CLIMATE

Prague sits in a landlocked country in central Europe. It tends to experience continental weather patterns springing from Russia, but can experience mild wet weather from the Atlantic. Winters are cold and wet but it has the capacity to be dry and clear for long spells. If the wind comes from Russia it can be extremely cold. Summers are warm but rainy with regular disturbances from the Mediterranean Sea to the south — June and July are two of the rainiest months of the year — with springs and falls marked with changeable weather.

		J	F	M	A	M	J	J	A	S	O	N	D
Maximum	°F	50	52	64	73	82	88	91	90	84	71	57	50
	°C	10	11	18	23	28	31	33	32	29	22	14	10
Minimum	°F	9	10	18	28	36	45	48	46	39	28	23	14
	°C	-13	-12	-8	-2	2	7	9	8	4	-2	-5	-10

CLOTHING

For most occasions casual comfortable clothing will be most practical in the city. In summer, lightweight clothing is recommended though one should always be prepared for a rain shower. Take a warm layer for cooler summer evenings. In spring and fall, a coat or heavy jacket is advisable. In winter take coat, hat, and gloves because continental winds can be bitterly cold and biting.

You will need comfortable shoes for strolling at all times of year, with sandals for the summer months.

If you want to attend formal performances such as opera or ballet, or perhaps eat in the finer restaurants, then a dressy ensemble would be appropriate. Although Prague is an informal city, its inhabitants do enjoy dressing formally on such occasions.

COMPLAINTS

Any complaints should be taken up with the organization concerned in the first instance. If you do not get satisfaction, contact the Prague Information Service at Na příkopě 20; Tel. 24 48 22 02. They should be able to advise you further.

CRIME AND SAFETY

Prague is a safe and pleasureable city to walk around. Violent crime is still relatively rare, however petty crime such as car theft and pick-pocketing has increased greatly with the rise in the number of visitors. Take the following precautions to reduce your risk of becoming a victim.

Leave valuables in the safe at your hotel.

Never carry large amounts of cash or flaunt expensive jewelry.

Carry valuables in inside pockets and keep purses close to your body.

Be aware in large crowds such as on Charles Bridge or in Wenceslas Square. Pick-pockets can be at work here.

Do not leave anything in vehicles.

Walk along well-lit streets at night.

I want to report a theft.	**Chci ohlásit krádež.**
My wallet/handbag/passport/ ticket has been stolen.	**Ukradli mi náprsní tašku (peněženku)/kabelku/pas/lístek.**

CUSTOMS AND ENTRY REQUIREMENTS

The Czech Republic is in constant consultation with other governments and the situation regarding customs and entry requirements is subject to change. At present the situation is as follows.

Visas. Citizens of the EU do not need a visa to enter the Czech Republic for up to 180 days. Citizens of the US, New Zealand, and South Africa can enter the Czech Republic on a visa waiver scheme for up to 90 days. Citizens of Canada can enter on visa waiver for up to 180 days.

Citizens of Australia need a visa to enter the Czech Republic. This must be obtained before you travel from the Czech Embassy. All travelers with visas must register with the Czech Immigration Police Service, though this will be done by your hotel. They will take your passport and visa details when you check in.

Vaccinations. You don't need vaccinations to enter the Czech Republic unless you are traveling from an infected area.

Currency Restrictions. There is no restriction on the amount of foreign currency you can import and export. In fact you must be able to prove if asked that you have access to 1,000 Kč per day or 37,000 Kč per month in order to be able to support yourself. In reality you are unlikely to be asked. There is an import and export limit of 5000 Kč for the Czech currency.

Keep your currency exchange receipts as you may be asked to show them, and you will certainly need them to change any remaining currency at the end of your stay.

Customs limitations. Travelers are allowed to import the following duty free goods.

200 cigarettes or 100 cigarillos or 50 cigars or 250 g of tobacco;
1 litre of spirits; 2 litres of wine;
50ml of perfume or 250 ml of eau de cologne.
You can also import gifts up to a value of 3000 Kč.
Visitors can import all reasonable items for personal use.
It is illegal to export antiques without a permit.

D

DRIVING

Road conditions. Road conditions in the Czech Republic are generally good, however signage is not so you need a good map to get around. Within Prague itself road conditions are also good but there are a number of cobbled roads in the downtown area as well as tramlines, both of which become slippery when wet. Complex one-way systems can be confusing.

Rules and Regulations. Drive on the right and pass on the left. Speed limits are 130 km/h (80 mph) on main highways, 90 km/h (56 mph) on secondary roads, and 60 km/h (37 mph) in urban areas. Seatbelts are compulsory where fitted in the vehicle and drunk driving is illegal. Drivers are generally level headed and patient, but do keep an extra watch out for trams and also pedestrians — many of these are tourists who are not familiar with the road layouts, etc. If you have an accident you must inform the police and wait for them to arrive before you move your vehicle.

Fuel costs. Fuel is cheap by European standards and is priced in litres. Diesel is around 24 Kč and premium unleaded fuel 32 Kč. Fuel stations are open from 8am–6pm, some are open later. Most of the international fuel stations — such as Aral — take credit cards, however owner-operators may not. Make sure you ask before you fill your tank if you don't have enough crowns to pay for your fuel.

Parking. Parking in the city poses some difficulties with reserved areas and numerous restrictions. A number of private wheel-clamping businesses operate in the city and you will be clamped if you infringe on parking regulations. On-street parking is divided into three zones; an orange zone is short term parking metered at 40 Kč per hour; a green zone is for stays of up to 6 hours, parking metered at 30 Kč per hour. Both of these zones have free parking on Sundays; Blue zones are for resident or company parking by permit only. The main guard-ed parking area for the city is next to the main railway station on Wilsonova but there are unguarded car parks under Wenceslas Square and near the Hotel Intercontinental in the Jewish Quarter.

If you need help. Dial 154 for the "yellow angels" or Autotourist Road Service. They will come out and attempt to repair your car or take you to the nearest garage. You will have to pay for this service. Dial 158 for the police.

Bringing your own car to Prague. You will need to carry the following items with you in addition to your valid drivers license — vehicle registration or ownership documents, a Green Card which extends your insurance, a national identity sticker, a first aid kit, a red warning triangle. Drivers must buy a road permit which is valid for one year. This can be purchased at the border crossing and must be on view in the windshield of your car. Current price 800 Kč. It would be wise to take out breakdown insurance. This can be obtained before you travel from your motoring organization. In the UK contact the AA, Tel. 0870 5500 600. In the US contact the AAA, Tel. (800) 222-4357 toll free.

Road signs:

Jednosměrný provoz	One way
Na silnici se pracuje	Road works (Men working)
Nebezpečí	Danger
Nevstupujte	No entry
Objížďka	Diversion (Detour)
Opatrně	Caution
Pěší zóna	Pedestrian zone
Pozor	Attention
Snižit rychlost (zpomalit)	Slow down
Vchod	Entrance
Východ	Exit

Full tank, please.	**Plnou nádrž, prosím.**
super/normal/unleaded/diesel	**super/obyčejný/ bezolovnatý/nafta**
Check the oil/tires/battery, please.	**Prosím, zkontrolujte mi olej/pneumatiky/baterii.**
I've broken down	**Mám poruchu.**
There's been an accident.	**Stala se nehoda.**
Can I park here?	**Mohu zde parkovat?**
Are we on the right road for …?	**Jedeme dobře do …? (Vede tato silnice do …?)**

E

ELECTRICITY

Prague uses the 220 volt, 50 cycle AC. Visitors will need adaptors (the same as French plugs) and travelers from the US will also need transformers for their equipment.

Prague

Web site <www.kropla.com/electric> gives information about the connections needed for all countries.

EMBASSIES/CONSULATES/HIGH COMMISSIONS

The following countries have diplomatic or consular representation in the Czech Republic.

US. Tržiště 15, Prague 1; Tel. 24 21 98 44.

Canada. Mickiewiczova 6, Prague 1; Tel. 24 31 11 08.

South Africa. Ruská 65, Prague1; Tel. 67 31 11 14.

Ireland. Tržiště 13, Prague 1; Tel. 53 09 02.

UK. Thunovská 14, Prague 1; Tel. 24 23 84 34.

New Zealand Consulate. Dykova 19, Prague 10; Tel. 22 51 46 72.

The nearest consular representation for the following country is in neighboring Austria.

Australia. 3rd floor, Winterhur House, Mattiellistrasse 2, Vienna A-1040; Tel. 43 1 512 8580.

EMERGENCIES

Contact the following emergency services by telephone 24 hours a day.

Police 158   Fire 150

First Aid/Medical 155

Fire!	**Hoří!**
Help!	**Pomoc!**
Stop thief!	**Chyt'te zloděje!**

G

GAY AND LESBIAN TRAVELERS

Gay and lesbian travelers will find Prague a welcoming destination. There is a lively gay scene with a number of clubs and bars to enjoy. Try Radnost (see What to Do) first and then move on to the latest hot venue.

GETTING THERE

By Air. Most people traveling to the city arrive by air and there are numerous flights daily from the major cities of Europe. Czech Airlines is the national carrier of the Czech Republic <www.csa.cz> and it operates direct flights to the following locations; New York in the US, though Czech Airlines also works in partnership with Continental Airlines to reach other cities; Toronto and Montreal in Canada; London and Manchester in the UK; Dublin in the Republic of Ireland.

No US carriers offer direct flights to Prague though Air Canada <www.aircanada.ca> has a service from Toronto.

The following airlines fly to Prague from London Heathrow and their own domestic hubs: British Airways, Air France (from Paris), KLM (from Amsterdam), Lufthansa (from Frankfurt and other major cities in Germany), Swissair (from Geneva), Austrian Air (from Vienna) and Alitalia (from Rome).

Connections from the US to Europe can be achieved with American Airlines, Delta Airlines, Continental Airlines, and Virgin Airlines. From Australia and New Zealand you can reach Europe for onward flights to Prague with Singapore Airlines, Thai Airlines, Quantas, and Air New Zealand.

By Rail. Eurorail <www.eurorail.com> has details of rail services throughout Europe. There are regular connections to Frankfurt or Vienna for onward connections. Prices for rail travel are cheap but traveling times are a little off-putting — 10 hours from Frankfurt. Information in English can be obtained from the main railway station in Prague, Tel. 24 22 38 87.

By road. (also see DRIVING) Eurolines operates buses that connect the major cities of Europe; web site <www.eurolines.com>.

GUIDES AND TOURS

There are numerous tours available in Prague and into the surrounding countryside. These include walking tours (individual and group), theme tours (perhaps musical or literary), horse-drawn carriage tours, little trains, and vintage car tours. These can be from 30 minutes to a whole day in length. Registered English-speaking guides can be hired by the hour by individuals or groups. Contact Čedok or Prague Information Service for more information.

If you want to take a trip to nearby castles or towns there are a number of companies who provide organized coach tours with or without lunch. Prague Sightseeing Tours have a comprehensive program and can be contacted at Klimentská 52, Prague 1; Tel. 231 46 61; fax 231 80 17; web site <www.vol.cx/pst>.

H

HEALTH AND MEDICAL CARE

There are no major health concerns when visiting the Czech Republic. However, foreign visitors must pay for all medical treatment except emergency treatment, so make sure that you travel with adequate health and accident insurance. You may have to pay in cash and reclaim the cost on your return home, so have spare capacity on your credit card or extra travelers' checks to cover minor problems.

A number of medical facilities cater specifically to visitors and you will be sure to find English-speaking medical personnel to help you.

For minor health problems Prague has modern pharmacies (lékárna) including one 24-hour facility at Štefánikova 6. Though the range of drugs available is not as wide as in Western Europe or the US, you will still be able to find remedies for most common travelers' ailments.

The Diplomatic Health Centre for foreigners (Na Homolce) is located at Roentgenova 2, Prague 5; Tel. 52 92 11 11.

The American Medical Centre can be found at Janovského 48, Prague 7; Tel. 80 77 56.

For first aid visit Fakulní Poliklinika at U nemocnice 2 in the New Town; Tel. 24 22 25 20.

HITCHHIKING

Hitchhiking is not illegal in the Czech Republic, however it is an inherently dangerous form of travel. Women traveling alone should take extra care, especially as a small number of prostitutes operate on the major highways leading into Europe and drivers may misinterpret the intentions of a single woman hitchhiker waiting alone at the roadside.

HOLIDAYS

The following dates are national holidays in the Czech Republic, when all official offices and banks will be closed.

1 January	*Nový rok*	New Year's Day
1 May	*Svátek práce*	May Day
8 May	*Vítěztví nad fašismum*	Victory over fascism
5 July	*Slovanští věrozvěsti sv. Cyril a Metoděj*	Slavic Missionaries St. Cyril and St. Methodius
6 July	*Výročí úmrtí Jana Husa*	The anniversary of Jan Hus's death
28 October	*První československá republika*	First Czechoslovak Republic
24 December	*Štědrý den*	Christmas Eve
25–26 December	*Svátek vánoční*	Christmas/Boxing Day
Movable date	*Velikonoční pondělí*	Easter Monday

L

LANGUAGE

The national language is Czech. The most widely studied foreign languages are English and German. If Slavic languages are Greek to you, don't worry—English is widely spoken, though an understanding of German may help. If you can learn a few Czech words, it will always be appreciated.

The Czech alphabet has 33 letters; for instance, *c* and *č* are counted as two different letters. Here are a few tips on the pronunciation of the more difficult sounds:

ť like *ty* in no**t y**et

ň like the *n* in Ca**n**ute

š like the *sh* in **sh**ine

ž like the *s* in plea**s**ure

c like *ts* in **ts**etse

č like *ch* in **ch**urch

ch like English *h*

j like *y* in **y**ellow

ř like *rs* in Pe**rs**ian

The Berlitz Czech Phrase Book and Dictionary covers most situations you are likely to encounter during your visit to the Czech Republic.

Do you speak English?	**Mluvíte anglicky?**
I don't speak Czech.	**Nemluvím česky.**
Good morning/Good afternoon	**Dobré jitro/Dobré odpoledne**
Good evening/Good night	**Dobrý večer/Dobrou noc**
Please	**Prosím**
Thank you	**Děkuji Vám**
Thank you very much	**Velice Vám děkuji**
That's all right/You're welcome.	**To je v pořádku.**

LAUNDRY AND DRY CLEANING

Most major hotels offer a laundry service but this can be expensive. There are few commercial laundries (*prádelna*) or dry cleaners (*čistírna*) in the city, however Laundry Kings at Dejvická 16 (Tel. 312 37 43), next to the Hradcanska metro station, is open daily until 10pm. Laundryland at Londýnská 71, Prague 2 (Tel. 25 11 24), near to I.P. Pavlova metro station, also has repair and alteration services.

M

MAPS

Čedok and the Prague Information Service both produce maps that are helpful in touring the city. Some hotels also provide a map as part of their welcome package. For a comprehensive commercial map the Prague city map printed by Bema Praha is readily available in shops in the city and makes a useful companion for traveling by foot or on public transport.

MEDIA

TV: Most major hotels have cable or satellite TV in each room with one or more English-speaking news channels. The major ones are CNN, BBC 24, and Sky News. Foreign broadcasts on Czech TV are dubbed rather than subtitled, though there may be English-speaking programs on other foreign service TV stations.

Radio: Radio Praha on frequency 101.1 FM broadcasts news in English three times each day. They can also be accessed at their web site <www.radio.cz>.

Press: All the main foreign-language newspapers are available at newsstands in the city. There are also several English publications printed locally and aimed at visitors to the city. *ThePraguePost* contains news and comment as well as listing local events. It is published weekly. There are also *This Month in Prague* and *Prague Guide*, two small monthly publications. These highlight cultural events taking place each month but also include information on shopping, hotels, etc.

MONEY

The currency of the Czech Republic is the crown or *koruna* (Kč). Each crown is made up of 100 hellers (hal.). Currency is issued in notes of 5,000 Kč, 2,000 Kč, 1,000 Kč, 500 Kč, 200 Kč, 100 Kč, 50 Kč, 20 Kč and coins of 50 Kč, 20 Kč, 10 Kč, 5 Kč, 2 Kč, 1 Kč, and 50 hellers, 20 hellers and 10 hellers.

Currency Exchange. There are many private banks and exchange bureaus in the city. Banks are open from 8am–4pm and many close their exchange facilities at lunch time. They charge a standard 1% commission. Exchange bureaus have much more flexible hours, often open until 10pm, but can charge up to 10% commission, so it pays to shop around. Hotels will also change currency but their commission rates vary.

If you want to exchange your remaining crowns back to your own currency before you leave the Czech Republic, you must have an official receipt for your original currency exchange. Beware of black market currency traders. It is illegal to exchange currency in this fashion, and it is often a way of introducing counterfeit notes into the system.

Credit Cards. Credit cards are increasingly accepted for payment throughout the city. They are now accepted by the majority of hotels, but it still pays to ask about credit card payments before ordering in restaurants or choosing objects in stores if this is your only method of payment.

ATMs. There are an increasing number of international ATMs in the city that will issue cash against your current account card or credit card. Look for the Cirrus or Plus sign on the machine. Some major hotels also have machines in their foyers.

Travelers' Checks. Travelers' checks are a safe way of carrying cash and can be exchanged at banks: Stay with the major issuers. However, they will not be accepted as payment in shops, restaurants or hotels.

O

OPEN HOURS
Banks are open 8am–4pm (some close from noon–1pm) Monday–Friday. Exchange bureaus operate every day, staying open until 10pm or later.

General stores may open as early as 6am and department stores open at 8am. Both close at around 6pm, and will be closed on Sunday.

Tourist stores open at 9am and can remain open until 9pm. Many open seven days per week.

Museums open from 10am–6pm. Many close on Sundays with the exception of the Synagogues, which are closed on Saturday.

P

PLANNING YOUR TRIP ON THE WEB

The web sites for organizations mentioned throughout this book are included with their contact details, however here are a few web sites that may be of help in the research and planning of your trip. They also offer links to other sites.

<www.praguepost.cz> The online information of the English printed *Prague Post* newspaper.

<www.prague.com>

<www.pragueiguide.com>

<www.czech-travel-guide.com>

POLICE

There are several types of security forces operating in the city. State police are responsible for day-to-day policing. They wear white shirts and dark grey slacks or skirts. They are armed.

Municipal police wear light grey slacks or skirts.

Traffic police are responsible for all roads and traffic regulations. They may erect roadblocks to check papers (always carry your driver's license and passport as well as your car papers) or to breathalyze drivers — any amount of alcohol on the breath will result in severe punishment. This police force also controls fines for parking and clamping infringements. If you are involved in a traffic accident you must inform the police before moving your vehicle.

Finally there are an increasing number of private security personnel who work for banks, etc. They have no community remit but are armed. They will wear black or blue uniforms.

The emergency number for the police service is 158.

POST OFFICES

Postal services are cheap and reliable for sending letters and post-cards. Most shops that sell postcards will also sell stamps, as will a lot of hotels.

The main post office is at Jindřišská 14, just off Wenceslas Square. It is open 24 hours a day. Here you can send telegrams and make international calls as well as buy stamps and phonecards. If you only want postal services, buy your stamps elsewhere because this place is huge with over 50 counters, each of which has a special function.

Postal rates: 7 Kč for stamp to Europe, 10 Kč for further afield, however there have been several price increases in recent years so this is likely to change more quickly than other prices.

Mail boxes are either orange with side slit (old style) or orange-and-blue with a front flap (new style).

PUBLIC TRANSPORTATION

Prague has a comprehensive and integrated public transport system that provides a cheap and efficient service. Tickets and passes can be used on all forms of transport.

Each ticket has a time limit and you pay more for a longer time limit. The cheapest ticket: 8 Kč allows 15 minutes of travel with no transfer or 4 stops on the metro with no line change. A 12 Kč ticket allows 60 minutes of travel and allows line change or tram transfer within that time. Children aged between 6 and 15 must pay half price.

Tickets can be bought at metro stations (there are automatic ticket machines which give instructions in English, and supply change) or newsstands. They must be validated when you step on the tram or arrive at the metro station. You will see small yellow machines into which you must insert your ticket.

Day tickets or longer passes are also available and are valid for unlimited travel on all forms of transport. These can often be supplied by your hotel concierge but can be purchased at the M.H.D. kiosks at all major metro stations. They will be valid from the date stamped on them and do not have to be validated for each journey. Prices are as follows.

Twenty four hour pass 70 Kč

Three day pass 180 Kč

Seven day pass 250 Kč

Fifteen day pass 280 Kč

Trams. There is a comprehensive network of 31 tram routes, which operate and connect both sides of the river. Each tram stop shows the tram number passing there and a timetable. Most city maps show the tram routes in addition to the location of the major attractions. It would help to purchase one of these (see section on maps above). All trams run from 4:30am–midnight, but a number of routes are also designated as night routes and will operate a service 24 hours per day. Purchase your ticket before you travel and validate it as you enter unless you are transferring from another tram or metro within your allotted time.

Metro. The extremely efficient Prague metro opened in 1974 and provides a great service for visitors. There are three interlinked lines and metro maps can be found at each station. Metro signs above ground feature a stylized M incorporated into an arrow pointing downwards. Metro trains operate until midnight.

Bus. Buses tend to operate out to the Prague suburbs rather than compete with trams in the city.

Funicular at Petřín. The ride to the top of Petřín Hill also takes standard tickets. You can purchase these at the station just before you travel.

Taxis. Most complaints from visitors about trips to Prague tend to be about taxi journeys. Since deregulation in 1989 taxis are now operated by private companies, and there are unscrupulous operators out there. Prices are supposed to be 25 Kč then 17 Kč per kilometer with an additional charge of 4 Kč per minute at busy times. There are also extra charges for baggage and the prices rise by up to 300% at night. It may be wise to negotiate a price for the journey before you enter the taxi rather than rely on the meter.

A reputable firm with staff who speak some English is AAA Taxis (Tel. 312 21 22).

R

RELIGION

The Czech Republic is mainly a Catholic country and Prague has a profusion of beautiful churches that still hold regular services. Some also hold services in English. Times will be posted outside the individual church, or consult the Prague Post (see Media above). Within the city there is an active Jewish community and there are also Anglican and Baptist churches.

T

TELEPHONE

Note: The whole telephone system in the Czech Republic is undergoing a thorough upgrade and overhaul and there will be number changes in the coming years as demand is expected to rise exponentially. All telephone numbers throughout this guide are current at time of printing, but if you do have problems reaching a number, the Prague directory enquiries number is 120. They have some English-speaking staff.

Although it is possible to use street phone boxes to make international calls, in practice the service is still in its infancy and you will have more success from a post office (you pay a deposit to start your call and then pay the balance when you have finished) or through your hotel — though they will add a high surcharge for the service. Some hotels will provide details of international access numbers to organizations such as AT&T. These allow you to make direct international calls at lower rates provided you pay by credit card. The international operator can be contacted on 0132.

Public phones take phone cards (*telefonní karta*). These can be bought at Post Offices or newsstands.

Cybercafés. There are a number of cafés in the city offering Internet access. This is certainly a good option for keeping in touch when compared to both the price and system reliability of making phone calls.

The international code for the Czech Republic is 420 with a Prague city code of 2, which must de dialled from outside the country. To ring Prague from outside the city dial 02.

To call the following countries from Prague dial 00, then one of the following codes.

United States 1	United Kingdom 44	Ireland 353
Canada 1	South Africa 27	New Zealand 64
Australia 61		

TICKETS

There is no central ticket office for events in Prague. Visit each individual box office for event tickets, buy from one of the roving ticket sellers in the main square, or visit the Prague Information Service (PIS) office — see Tourist Information below. However be aware that prices are often cheaper if you buy tickets direct from the box office.

TIME ZONES

Prague operates on Central European Time (CET). This is one hour ahead of GMT in winter and 2 hours ahead of GMT in summer.

When it is noon in Prague,

London	New York	Jo'burg	Sydney	Auckland
11am	6am	11am	8pm	10pm

TIPPING

Tipping is appreciated but levels are low and in some restaurants, service is included in the price — it should state this on the menu.

For other services tips should be as follows.

Leave small change in a bar.

Waiter 10%

Taxi driver 10%

Tour guide 60 Kč.

Hotel porter 15 Kč per bag.

Chambermaid 15 Kč per day/60 Kč per week.

TOILETS

There are public toilets at each metro station, which should remain open until 9pm. You should leave some small change 1 or 2 Kč.

If you don't see the symbol denoting a man or woman, ladies' toilets will be labelled *Ženy* or *Dámy*, mens' will be *Muži* or *Páni*.

TOURIST INFORMATION

For information before you leave for Prague contact Čedok Tourist Agency which was the government tourist office but has now been privatized. They have offices in the following locations.

UK. Čedok. 95 Great Portland Street, London W1N 5RA. Tel; 020 7291 9920, fax; 020 7436 8300

US. Čedok. 1109-1111 Madison Avenue, New York, N.Y. 10028. Tel; (212) 288 0830, fax; (212) 288 0971

Canada. Čedok. P.O. Box 198, Exchange Tower 14th Floor. 2, First Canada Place, Toronto. Ontario M5X 1A6. Tel; (416) 367 3432, fax; (416) 367 3492.

There are many commercial agencies offering tourist information and selling tours, etc. Here are the addresses of two reliable organizations within Prague that have proved to be both longstanding and professional. Čedok. Na příkopě. 18, Prague 1; Tel. 24 19 71 11. Rytířská 16, Prague 1; Tel. 26 27 14. They also have web site at <www.cedok.cz>.

Prague Information Service. Na příkopě 20, Prague 1; Tel. 26 40 22. Staroměstské náměstí 1, Prague 1; Tel. 24 48 22 02.

W

WEIGHTS AND MEASURES

The Czech Republic uses the metric system.

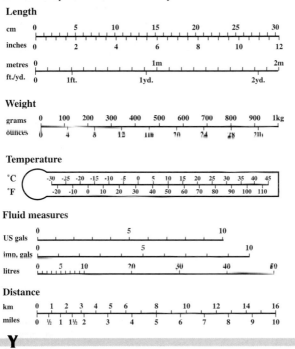

Length

Weight

Temperature

Fluid measures

Distance

Y

YOUTH HOSTELS

Contact the C.K.M. (Youth Travel Bureau) at Žitná 12; Tel. 29 12 40; fax 24 21 62 10. They are open between 8am and 6pm for information. Juniorhotel is also on the same site, offering basic rooms.

Recommended Hotels

Since the "Velvet Revolution" Prague has become one of the most popular tourist cities in Europe and there has been a tremendous growth in the number of rooms available. There are numerous newly built hotels, but many date from the communist era and although they offer up-to-date facitlities, they do have a rather dour exterior design. However, the city does have a number of gems including beautiful Art Nouveau hotels and other older, historic buildings. Accomodation is expensive in relation to the other costs of your stay and there is still a lack of good budget value accomodations. There are few family-owned small hotels that are featured in other European destinations, though the situation is improving every year. It is always preferable to have a confirmed room reservation before you arrive in Prague, especially during the peak seasons — June–September and around Christmas time. Rates will be quoted per room per night and may be in Deutsch Marks rather than crowns. Room rates may not include room taxes of 22% and a small municipal tax, so always make specific enquiries about a tax before you make a booking. Breakfast is not always included and in top-class hotels could add 800 to 1,000 crowns to the cost of your night's stay. Disabled access is variable and generally better in the more modern hotels. Always make detailed enquiries about facilities if this is important for you.

The following hotel recommendations cover all areas of the city, including large and small hotels with local and international management.

If telephoning Prague from outside the Czech Republic dial 00+420+2 before the following numbers.

$$$$$	over 6,000 Kč
$$$$	5,000–6,000 Kč
$$$	4,000–5,000 Kč
$$	3,500–4,000 Kč
$	under 3,000Kč

OLD TOWN AND NEW TOWN

The Palace $$$$$ *Panská 12, 110 00 Prague 1; Tel. 24 09 31 11; fax 24 22 12 40.* Situated close to Wenceslas Square, the refurbished Palace is arguably the most luxurious and the most expensive hotel in the city. The décor is extravagant and lavish with service aimed to provide everything a tourist would need. Rooms have A/C, TV, phone, safe, mini-bar, hair dryer. Facilities include restaurant, bar, 24-hour room service. Access for disabled guests. Parking at extra charge. 125 rooms. Major credit cards.

Radisson SAS $$$$$ *Štěpánská 40, 110 00 Prague 1; Tel. 22 82 00 00; fax. 22 82 01 00; web site <www.radisson.com>.* Radisson has updated and renovated this renowned 1930s hotel on a main street just off Wenceslas Square. Beautifully furnished throughout, the rooms have A/C, TV, safe, phone/fax/PC point, mini-bar, tea and coffee, hair dryer, trouser press. Some rooms with kitchenettes. Facilities include restaurant, bar, fitness room, sauna, solarium, 24-hour room service, shop. Parking at extra charge. 10 rooms equipped for disabled guests. 211 rooms. Major credit cards.

Hotel Paříž $$$$$ *U Obecniho Domu 1, 110 00 Prague 1; Tel. 22 19 56 66; fax 24 22 54 75; web site <www.hotel-pariz.cz>.* The Hotel Paříž, situated next to Municipal House, was one of Prague's finest establishments when it was built in 1904. Today it has been totally refurbished and is once again at its dazzling best, with stunning interiors and elegant if ornate façade. If you don't stay here, visit the Café de Paris for a drink. Rooms have A/C, TV, phone/PC point, safe, mini-bar, hair dryer, robes. Facilities include gourmet restaurant, bar/café, fitness room/spa, 24-hour room service. 88 rooms. Major credit cards.

Hotel President $$$$ *náměstí Curieových 100, 116 88 Prague 1; Tel. 231 48 12; fax 231 82 47.* Offering superb views across the Vlatva towards the castle, the President is the epitome of Prague's old-style hotels. Built in the 1970s, its rather sombre exterior hides interior spaces which have been thoroughly updated. Popular with tour groups. Rooms have TV, phone, mini-bar, safe. Facilities include restaurant, roof terrace with views over the river. 97 rooms. Major credit cards.

Hotel Adria $$$ *Václavské náměstí (Wenceslas Square) 26, 110 00 Prague 1; Tel. 24 21 65 43; fax 24 21 10 25.* This newly refurbished hotel is bright and welcoming with pretty rooms and communal areas. Perfectly placed for touring and enjoying the nightlife. Rooms have TV, phone, room service. Facilities include restaurant, bar. Wheelchair access. 66 rooms. Major credit cards.

Ungelt $$$$ *Štupartská 1, Prague 1; Tel. 24 81 13 30; fax 231 95 05.* A very central hotel situated just off the Old Town Square, the Ungelt offers simple but stylish accommodations, some suites with kitchenettes. The buildings were part of an old medieval warehouse. There is a terrace in summer, which is used for parking in the winter. Suites have TV. Facilities include restaurant, bar, garden, room service. 16 suites. Major credit cards.

Atlantic Hotel $$ *Na poříčí 9, 110 00 Prague 1; Tel. 24 81 10 84; fax 24 81 23 78.* Located near Powder Tower, this small hotel makes a good base for enjoying the city on foot. The architecture is modern and a little lacking in character, but rooms are nicely furnished with TV and phone. Facilities include restaurant, bar/café. Rooms for disabled guests. 61 rooms. Major credit cards.

Evropa Hotel $$ *Václavské náměstí (Wenceslas Square) 25, 118 00 Prague 1; Tel. 42 22 81 17; fax 24 22 45 44.* The Art Nouveau masterpiece has been one of Prague's highlights during the 20th century. The interior still retains the original decoration, which has not yet been "over-renovated." This gives the Evropa an air of the real Prague — an aging elegance if a little faded. Rooms vary greatly in size and facilities but this is the place to stay to capture the emotional heart of the Prague of yesteryear. Ask for a room with bathroom when you make a booking. Facilities include restaurant, bar. 89 rooms. Major credit cards.

CASTLE AREA AND LESSER QUARTER.

Hotel Hoffmeister $$$$–$$$$$ *Pod Broskou 7, Klárov, 118 00 Prague 1; Tel. 510 17 111; fax 510 17 120; web site <www.hoffmeister.cz>.* This family-owned and -operated hotel is situated near the foot of the Staré zámecké schody (Old castle steps) and is less than five minutes' walk from Malostranská metro station. Each room is individually and well-furnished including original art created by Adolf Hoffmeister, father of the present owner. Rooms have A/C, TV, phone, mini-bar. Facilities include gourmet restaurant, bar and pretty terrace. Parking at an extra charge. 32 rooms. Major credit cards.

U Raku $$$$$ *Černínská 10, Hradčany, 118 00 Prague 1; Tel. 205 111 00; fax 205 105 11.* In the quiet residential area of Novy Svet, near Prague Castle, this small luxury hotel — located in a wood lath, cottage-style building that is a national monument — makes the perfect romantic getaway. Rooms and communal areas are equipped to a high standard with original paintings by the artist owners. The rooms range around a small courtyard and there are pretty terraced gardens. Rooms have TV. 6 rooms. Major credit cards.

Savoy $$$$ *Keplarova 6, 118 00 Praha 1; Tel. 24 30 24 20; fax 24 30 21 28; web site <www.hotel-savoy.cz>.* Located near the Loreta, Strahov Monastery, and Prague Castle, the Savoy also has a tram connection into town outside its door. The rooms are spacious and have A/C, satellite TV, safe, phone/fax/PC point, hair dryer, robes, complimentary mini-bar with wine, beer, and soft drinks. Facilities include complimentary "relax center" with sauna, spa and fitness equipment, restaurant, bar, 24-hour room service. Rooms specially equipped for the disabled. Parking available at extra charge. 55 rooms. Major credit cards.

U Tří pštrosů $$$ *Dražického náměstí 12, 118 00 Prague 1; Tel. 24 51 07 79; fax 24 51 07 83.* Situated in a small square at the Mala Stranma end of Charles Bridge, U Tří pštrosů is perfectly situated for exploring the town on foot, and offers an intimate family atmosphere. The hotel name means "At the Three Ostriches" because the original owner of the house imported ostrich feathers. Rooms have TV. Facilities include good restaurant, bar. Parking at extra charge. 18 rooms. Major credit cards.

Hotel Sax $$$ *Janský Vršek 3, Malá Strana, 118 00 Prague 1; Tel. 575 31 268; fax 575 34 101.* A couple of minutes from the main square of Malá Strana and very near the US embassy, the Hotel Sax is a new hotel behind a classical façade. The rooms, set around an atrium, are simply furnished but clean. They have TV and phone. Facilities include a bar. 22 rooms. Major credit cards.

Kampa $–$$$ *Všehrdova 16, 118 00 Prague 1; Tel. 24 51 04 09; fax 24 51 03 77.* A new hotel housed in what was originally an old armory, the Kampa offers excellent value for its position in the Lesser Quarter, only minutes by foot from Charles Bridge. Rooms are simply furnished but the hotel has good facilities for the price. These include a restaurant, bar, and garden. 85 rooms. Major credit cards.

A LITTLE FURTHER AFIELD

Corinthia Towers $$$$$ *Kongresová 1, 140 69 Prague 4; Tel. 61 19 11 11; fax 61 21 16 73; web site <www.corinthia.com>.* Sitting atop one of Prague's hills with magnificent views across the city and only a few meters to Vyšehrad metro station, the Corinthia Towers is Prague's newest 5-star hotel thanks to recent renovations. Rooms have A/C, cable TV, safe, phone, hair dryer, mini-bar, robes. Facilities include three restaurants, bar, café, casino, 24-hour room service, pool, fitness room and spa, bowling. Parking and valet parking at extra charge. Rooms specially equipped for wheelchair users. 531 rooms. Major credit cards.

Corinthia Panorama $$$$ *Milevská 7, 140 63 Prague 4; Tel. 61 16 11 11; fax 61 16 41 41; web site <www.corinthia.com>.* This large hotel is situated a couple of minutes' walk from Pankrác metro station — three stops from Wenceslas Square. Refurbished in 1996 the rooms now have A/C, cable TV, phone, in-room fax/PC connection, mini-bar, hair dryer, bathrobe. Facilities include restaurants, bar, coffee shop, casino, fitness center with sauna and spa, business center. Breakfast included in the price. Parking and valet parking at extra charge. 417 rooms. Major credit cards.

Club Hotel Praha $$$–$$$$$ *Průhonice 400. Tel. 74 01 07 41; fax 67 75 00 64; web site <club-hotel-praha.cz>.* Found a 20-minute ride out of the city just off the D1 ring road, Club Hotel has a large sports facility with tennis courts, squash, badminton, and bowling. Set on large, forested lot. Rooms have TV, phone, mini-bar, hair dryer. Other facilities include restaurant, bar, fitness center, pool, sauna, solarium, parking. Shuttle bus to the downtown area. 100 rooms. Major credit cards.

Golf Motol $–$$$ *Plzeňská 215, Prague 5; Tel. 52 32 51; fax 52 21 53.* You'll find this motel on the Plzeň road at the junction of the D1 ring road. Rooms are basic motel-style with TV and phone but the real draw is the neighboring golf course. Facilities include restaurant and bar. 40 rooms. Major credit cards.

Recommended Restaurants

Food is still very affordable in Prague despite several price increases in recent years. Most restaurants accept people walking in off the street. If you want to eat at a particular establishment it would be better to make a reservation, particularly at weekends and during high season. All but the finest restaurants accept casual dress.

Several charges can be added to your bill. A cover charge is automatic, along with a charge for any pre-appetizers. At budget establishments you may also be charged for condiments, which can bring the price to the level of better quality eateries. Tax (22%) may also be added but could be included in the price, so ask about extra charges before you order if you are on a budget. Although credit cards are more widely accepted than ever before, they are not universally accepted.

Most restaurants will close between lunch and dinner; where food is served without a break this will be advertised as "non-stop." Lunch is generally between 11am–3pm and dinner 6:30pm–10:30pm. Check with each individual establishment for exact times.

The following selection of restaurants includes establishments in all price brackets and features a range of cuisine with many Czech and some international restaurants. Indicated prices are for a three-course dinner per person without drinks. If you wish to make a reservation from outside the Czech Republic dial 00+420+2 before the numbers below.

$$$$$	over 1000 Kč
$$$$	700–1000 Kč
$$$	500–700 Kč
$$	300–500 Kč
$	under 300 Kč

OLD AND NEW TOWN

La Perle de Prague $$$$$ *Tančící dům, Rašínovo nábřeží 80; Tel. 21 98 41 60.* Located at the top of the "Fred and Ginger" building, La Perle de Prague offers wonderful views over the city from the indoor tables and the rooftop terrace, and has great modern décor. You'll find a great range of French dishes here including a great cheeseboard. Open daily for lunch noon–2pm, dinner 7pm–10:30pm. Reservations recommended. Major credit cards.

U staré Synagogy $$$$ *Pařížská 17; Tel. 231 85 52.* In the heart of the Jewish Quarter of Josefov, this new restaurant/café makes a good attempt at recreating an old-fashioned eatery. Traditional Czech cuisine. Some sidewalk tables. Great for lunch or dinner. Open daily 11:30am–midnight.

U Modré Růže $$$$ *Rytířská 16; Tel. 26 10 81.* "The Red Rose" is situated in one of the many valted cellars in Prague dating back to the 15th century and just around the corner from the M?stek metro station. The elegant décor is matched by a mixture of classical Czech and continental dishes — both meat and seafood, along with new ingredients such as ostrich steak. Open Mon–Sat 11:30am–11.30pm, Sun 6pm–11:30pm. Major credit cards.

Rybí Trh $$$–$$$$ *Týn 5; Tel. 42 89 54 47.* Found in the shadow of Our Lady of Týn church, this restaurant serves only fish dishes. Fresh fish, lobster, and other seafood is flown in daily to allow you the widest choice, which is then cooked to your precise requirements. Pretty outdoor terrace for summer dining. Open daily 11am–midnight. Major credit cards.

Bellevue $$$$ *Smetanovo nábřeží 2; Tel. 24 22 13 87.* The Bellevue has exactly what it says; situated near the Smetena Museum it has beautiful views across the river Vlatva. The interior is also visually spectacular with Art Deco decoration. The menu is mostly international — the owner is English — so it may make a change from Czech cuisine. Sunday buffet. Open daily for lunch noon–3pm, dinner 5:30pm–11pm. Major credit cards.

Red Hot n'Blues $$$ *Jakubská 12; Tel. 231 46 39*. This is where the US ex-pat community meets for BBQs, steaks, Creole dishes such as étouffé and chowder, along with real burgers. Seafood and salads are also on the menu. There is a weekend brunch and live music — you guessed it, blues — every evening. Come here for breakfast if you don't want to eat in your hotel. Open daily 9am–11pm. Major credit cards.

Buffalo Bills $$–$$$ *Vodičkova 9; Tel. 24 94 86 24*. The best in Tex-Mex cuisine, New Mexican décor, and country music makes this a relaxing and fun place to eat. Also some vegetarian entrées. Situated on a main street leading off Wenceslas Square. Open daily noon–midnight. Major credit cards.

The Taj Mahal $$–$$$ *Škrétova 10; Tel. 24 22 55 66*. Centrally located in the streets behind the National Museum, just off Wenceslas Square, the Taj Mahal offers a great range of authentic Indian dishes from marinated tikka to curry. Live Indian music makes a great accompaniment to your meal. Open Mon–Sat noon–11:30pm, Sun 3pm–11pm. Major credit cards.

U Bílé Krávy $$–$$$ *Rubešova 10; Tel. 24 23 95 70*. "At the White Cow" is an apt name for this restaurant where the owner also farms his own animals, Charolais cattle from Burgundy in France. He provides information about his meat so you can be sure that it's fresh and natural. Situated in the streets behind the National Museum, the restaurant presents country-French cuisine in a country-French setting, including frog's legs and snails among others — delicious and great value. Open daily 11am–11pm. Major credit cards.

U Fleků $$ *Křemencová 11, Prague 1; Tel. 24 91 51 18.* The oldest brewery in the city dating from 1499, you can enjoy U Flek dark beer, which is still brewed on the premises, along with hearty Czech food. Great beer hall atmosphere with live music and other performances. Outside courtyard. Located near Charles Square in the New Town. Open daily 9am–11pm. Major credit cards.

Country Life $–$$ *Melantrichova 15; Tel. 24 21 33 66.* Another self-service vegetarian eatery, it is one of the few places in the city also offering vegan dishes. Non-smoking dining room. Open Mon–Thur 9am–9pm, Fri 9am–4pm, Sun 11am–9pm. Cash only.

Kmotra Pizzeria $–$$ *V jirchářích 12; Tel. 24 91 58 09.* Situated in a vaulted basement in a street between the National Theatre and the New Town Hall, this café/pizzeria serves huge portions at budget prices so it's always busy with Prague citizens and tourists. Open daily 11am–1am. Cash only.

The Palace Hotel Cafeteria $–$$ *Panská 12; Tel. 235 75 56.* Said to be the best salad bar in town, and a great place to take a break from the meat-rich Czech cuisine. Self-service — but the food is good. Non-smoking dining room. Noon–9pm. Cash only.

U Kalicha $–$$ *Na Bojisti 12-14, Tel. 24 91 64 75.* At The Chalice is a historic pub/restaurant made famous because of the Czech novel *The Good Soldier Švejk*. The author Jaroslav Ha?ek made this bar his local and it, in turn, pays homage to him. There is a menu of Czech dishes and a lively sing-along. A couple of minutes' walk from the I. P. Pavlova metro station. Open daily 11am–11pm, reservations advisable in the evenings. Major credit cards.

CASTLE AREA AND LESSER QUARTER

U Malířů $$$$$ *Maltézské náměstí 11; Tel. 57 53 00 00.* This is said to be the most expensive restaurant in Prague — though by international price scales it still offers value for money. This restaurant sits on a quiet square in the Lesser Quarter. French haute cuisine in a beautiful 15th-century dining room complete with elaborately decorated ceiling; also a tiny outside terrace. Perfect for that special occasion. Open daily dinner only 7pm–11pm. Major credit cards.

Nebozízek $$$–$$$$ *Petřínské sady 411; Tel. 53 79 05.* Located halfway up the Petřín cablecar, this restaurant offers panoramic views across the city with a large terrace for summer dining. Mainly Czech dishes but you'll also find Chinese food. Open daily 11am–6pm and 7pm–11pm. Closed on Mondays in winter. Reservations recommended. Major credit cards.

U Modré Kachničky $$$–$$$$ *Nebovidská 6; Tel. 57 32 03 80.* "At the Blue Duckling," furnished with antiques and having walls decorated with Art Nouveau images, the restaurant is famed for its meat, fish, and game dishes and is extremely popular with the people of Prague. Situated in a street off Maltézské náměstí. Open daily noon–4pm, 6:30pm–11:30pm. Major credit cards.

U Vladaře $$$–$$$$ *Maltézské náměstí 10; Tel. 57 53 41 21.* In business since 1779, this restaurant sits on a quiet square in the Lesser Quarter. There are several vaulted dining areas and a pretty outside terrace. Traditional Czech dishes with some international cuisine. Open daily. Major credit cards.

U Zlaté Hrušky $$$–$$$$ *Nový svět 3; Tel. 20 51 47 78.* Found in one of the most beautiful and peaceful areas of the city, this restaurant — At the Golden Bear in English — is one of the most popular cellar-type eateries with low lighting and a traditional Czech menu. It has a pretty summer garden. Open daily lunch 11:30am–3pm, dinner 4pm–midnight in summer, 6pm–midnight in winter. Major credit cards.

David $$$ *Tržiště 21; Tel. 57 53 31 09*. Situated near the US embassy, below Prague Castle, David's simple white walls, modern art, and classical music form the backdrop to the elegant cuisine served here. It's popular with business people at lunch times. Czech and international dishes. Open daily 11:30am–11pm. Major credit cards.

U sv. Tomáše $$–$$$ *Letenská 12; Tel. 53 16 32*. At St. Thomas's is one of the traditional beer halls in the city. It was the earliest brewery in the city and connected to St. Thomas's Church next door (near the main square in the Lesser Quarter) but no longer brews its own beer. Great beer and good Czech food — including good roast meats — at large communal tables. Open daily 11:30am–11pm. Major credit cards.

Café Savoy $$ *Vítězná 1; Tel. 53 97 96*. Although not strictly a restaurant, this café in the southern area of the Lesser Quarter, is one of the most popular places in Prague to stop for refreshment. The beautiful setting, restored murals and classical music create a relaxed yet genteel ambiance. Open daily 9am–11pm. Major credit cards.

A LITTLE FURTHER AFIELD

Rickshaw Restaurant $$$–$$$$$ *Corinthia Towers Hotel. Tel. 61 19 11 11*. With a chef from Thailand and one from Laos, it is not surprising that this Oriental restaurant has dishes with the most authentic flavors. Portions are large so bring your appetite or some friends. Just steps from the Vyšehrad metro station. Open daily 6pm–11pm. Major credit cards.

Peklo $$$$ *Strahovské nádvoří 1; Tel. 57 32 01 09*. Situated in a small cave system behind Strahov Monastery and filled with antique furniture, Peklo means *hell* in Czech. The Italian owner offers a range of Czech and Italian dishes. You get great pasta here. Open daily for dinner only 7pm–midnight. Major credit cards.

INDEX